Hungry Hearts

Hungry Hearts

On Men, Intimacy, Self-Esteem, and Addiction

Joseph Nowinski

LEXINGTON BOOKS

An Imprint of Macmillan, Inc.
NEW YORK

Maxwell Macmillan Canada
TORONTO

Maxwell Macmillan International
NEW YORK • OXFORD • SINGAPORE • SYDNEY

Library of Congress Cataloging-in-Publication Data

Nowinski, Joseph.
    Hungry hearts : on men, intimacy, self-esteem, and addiction /
Joseph Nowinski.
        p. cm.
    Includes bibliographical references and index.
    ISBN 0–02–923221–X
    1. Compulsive behavior. 2. Men—Mental health. 3. Substance
abuse—Risk factors. I. Title.
    RC533.N68   1993
    616.86′0081—dc20   93–10681
                                                                         CIP

Lexington Books
An Imprint of Macmillan, Inc.
866 Third Avenue, New York, N.Y. 10022

Maxwell Macmillan Canada, Inc.
1200 Eglinton Avenue East
Suite 200
Don Mills, Ontario M3C 3N1

Macmillan, Inc. is part of the Maxwell Communication
Group of Companies.

Printed in the United States of America

printing number
1 2 3 4 5 6 7 8 9 10

For my father, who showed me the walk,
and for Kathleen, who taught me how to talk.

Contents

PART THREE
Men and Intimacy

Introduction

Addiction is arguably the most pressing and pervasive social problem facing American society today. Addiction can be generically defined as a compulsion either to use a mood-altering substance or to engage in a behavior (work, sex, gambling, eating, etc.). To qualify as an addiction, the use or behavior must meet two criteria: *tolerance,* meaning that over time the individual uses progressively more of the substance or engages more often in the behavior, but derives less satisfaction from it; and *loss of control,* meaning that over time the individual has experienced an inability to stop using the substance or engaging in the behavior.

More broadly, I consider a behavior an addiction when the individual is so *preoccupied* with it that it throws his or her life out of balance. An addiction—any addiction—takes on the qualities of a primary *relationship,* but a destructive one, not a productive one. The object of the relationship becomes a poor substitute for intimacy, self-confidence, and spirituality, but from the addict's perspective there is no other choice. Addiction is the result of emotional desperation, and it is this, as much as any physical craving, that drives addicts into relapse or leads them to substitute one addiction for another.

Using any definition of addiction, and including alcohol, drugs, sex, work, gambling, eating, and other behaviors on the list, it is difficult to estimate just how many Americans have an addiction of one kind or another. Similarly we have no idea how many multiply addicted individuals are out there, though we can probably assume that they are legion.

By far the most popular approach to dealing with addiction has been the "twelve-step" approach associated with Alcoholics Anonymous (AA).[1] It is estimated that more than 13 percent of the American population have attended a twelve-step group at least once, and that more than 5 percent have done so within the last year.[2] Over the past decade a broadly based twelve-step movement[3] has evolved, consisting of numerous "recovery" programs all modeled more or less loosely after AA. Obviously there is something in the twelve steps that has captured the attention of many troubled individuals, and that they find useful.

Although an increasing number of women have been getting involved in twelve-step programs,[4] the number of men who identify themselves as addicts is far larger. Attendance in AA, for example, remains about two-thirds male,[5] and the overall ratio of men to women enrolled in treatment programs for alcohol or drug abuse is roughly three to one.[6] In a survey of the population at large, men were five times as likely as women to be diagnosed as alcohol dependent.[7] It is probably safe to say that this sex difference holds across addictions. Among those fellowships that identify themselves as being for the *affected* (meaning partners of addicts), however, one is apt to find many more women in attendance.

This much, then, seems clear: addiction is a major social issue, and men appear to be considerably more predisposed than women to addictions of all kinds. The intriguing question, of course, is why? The various twelve-step fellowships have ventured tentative guesses at best, preferring to focus their efforts instead on the task of helping addicts stay sober one day at a time (through social support, combined with a loosely defined spirituality and much practical advice).

Of course, there is always the argument for a genetic factor underlying addiction. But that approach begs the question, since it amounts to saying merely that men are vulnerable to becoming obsessed because that is the way men are. And even if genetics played a role on such a grand scale, we would still need explanations that would account for whatever variance was not attributable to genes and would lend direction to efforts at treatment and prevention.

A second fact that must be considered is the high incidence of relapse among addicts. Between 60 and 70 percent of persons treated for addictions—including alcohol, nicotine, heroin, gambling, and overeating—relapse within the first year;[8] Within AA, only 40 percent of alcoholics who are sober and active in the fellowship for the first year will remain sober and active for a second year.[9] Data such as these point to our lack of understanding of the origins of addiction.

In searching for clues to the social, psychological, and developmental factors underlying men's vulnerability to addiction, this book begins with the assumption that there are fundamentally two different orientations that can be taken toward oneself and the social world. The first orientation is a *hierarchical* one, in which the individual sees himself or herself in relation to others in terms of a hierarchy of some sort. One way that I can identify myself as a man, in other words, is through comparing and contrasting myself with others. Usually the hierarchies that men employ for this purpose are based on power or status: we establish (and then defend) a sense of how *relatively* rich, smart, athletic, attractive, clever, talented, righteous, and so forth we are in comparison to others. This way of viewing the social world and of anchoring oneself in relation to it has also been called a *positional* orientation.[10]

An alternative to the positional or hierarchical orientation is one in which the individual seeks not so much to compare and contrast as to *identify* and bond with others. From this perspective, the self is seen in terms of similarities and connections to others. Whereas the positional orientation is inherently given to competition, this alternative lends itself better to collaboration. And whereas the positional approach tends to separate and isolate the individual (as an inevitable consequence of comparing and contrasting), this other approach tends to connect the individual to others. This way of defining the self in relation to others has been called the *relational* orientation.[11]

For reasons that seem obvious, it has been suggested that men are inclined to take a positional orientation, whereas women are inclined to use a relational approach to establishing a sense of self.[12] I agree with this. Moreover, I will present a historical perspective on this issue of orientation toward self, which I see as linked to a social trend of gender divergence that became evident in the nineteenth century, peaked in the Victorian era, and went largely unchallenged until the middle of this century.

The thesis of this book is that men's greater vulnerability to addiction is attributable in part to the fact that men have been systematically socialized for nearly two centuries to define themselves and establish self-esteem by adopting a positional orientation. Beyond that, I will suggest that this orientation has set the stage for a view of men that has exaggerated their resilience and toughness while neglecting to appreciate their sensitivity. It is in fact a historical accident that men have come to be viewed as being insensitive, and it is a myth that they are emotionally tough. This view has inadvertently promoted the abuse and neglect of boys. This abuse and neglect, in combination with men's proclivity to take a positional orientation, contributes to the insecurity and isolation that drive men toward addiction.

This book will attempt to present a historical, social, and psychological perspective on men's vulnerability to addiction. As such it is neither inconsistent nor competitive with any existing views of addiction. To the contrary, I hope that it will offer a perspective that lends itself to treatment and especially to prevention. It is only if we thoughtfully reconsider our views of men and masculinity—of how men establish their identities and self-esteem, and how they can enhance their capacity for intimacy—that we will be able to reduce appreciably their vulnerability to addiction.

The material presented here is intended to help men who are in recovery to extend the boundaries of the growth to which recovery opens them. It may also help men who are not (or not yet) addicts avoid the pain of this disease. Beyond that, if this book helps men and women reconsider the assumptions that underlie how we have come to raise boys, then it will be truly worthwhile.

PART ONE

The Origins of Addiction

Almost without exception, alcoholics are tortured by loneliness. Even before our drinking got bad and people began to cut us off, nearly all of us suffered the feeling that we didn't quite belong.
—*from* Twelve Steps and Twelve Traditions[13]

In Narcotics Anonymous, we learn to share the loneliness, anger and fear that addicts have in common and cannot control.
—*from* Narcotics Anonymous[14]

1

Four Stories

Paul was the third of four children, one of twin sons born into an American family that lived on an island off the coast of South America. His father was the manager of an oil refinery in a town where oil was the only business and where Americans lived in their own colony, complete with schools and stores, churches and parks, and even a country club. The weather was warm, the sea was blue, and the white stucco house that Paul lived in glistened in the sun. It was a large, meandering house, fully staffed with a cook, two maids, and a full-time baby-sitter. The family could have easily afforded a chauffeur as well, except that Paul's father liked to drive. He was an important man, but a remote figure in Paul's life. Between work and civic commitments he was rarely home, and when he was he was not especially available.

In the midst of all these advantages Paul had one major liability. It seemed that his twin brother (a fair-haired, blue-eyed, and robust youth) closely resembled his mother's own brother, to whom she had been intensely attached but who had died in an accident when they were teenagers. Paul, meanwhile, was slender and angular, with brown hair and dark, intense eyes. His mother, who he realized much later had a drinking problem, provided for all of his physical needs well enough, and Paul liked to claim that she loved all of her children equally. To his wife, his siblings, and others who knew the family well, though, the truth was plain: it was Paul's brother who was the apple of his mother's eye and the true heir to the love she had felt for her brother. It was also Paul's brother who was the prime beneficiary of a wife's frustrated affection for her remote husband.

As early as kindergarten Paul began building a reputation for being inconsistent, rebellious, and aggressive. On the one hand, his teachers remarked that he was terribly bright and could be charming and affectionate; on the other hand, his motivation for schoolwork was decidedly lacking, his grades were spotty, and he frequently got into fights. Whenever he would come home bruised or bleeding, his mother would laugh and shake her head, bandage him up, and send him off. He could never recall her asking him how it happened that he got hurt so often. She never punished him that he could remember, but neither did she hug him or talk with him very much about his life growing up.

For as long as he could recollect, and considerably earlier than his male peers, Paul had been keenly interested in girls. In his own words, he would "obsess endlessly" about each one of his first crushes. Some of his clearest memories were about one particular girl he knew when he was thirteen. Her name was Kate, and she sat diagonally across the aisle from him in school that year. Even in the best of times Paul found it difficult to concentrate on schoolwork. That year he found it all but impossible. He was distracted by Kate's every move, riveted by her every word. If by chance their eyes ever met he could feel his face grow hot, his pulse quicken.

As Valentine's Day approached, Paul found himself becoming more and more agitated. His January report card was especially bad and included more than the usual number of comments about careless work and inattention, along with the usual notes about conflicts and veiled predictions of future disaster. But no one at home read them, and Paul himself could not care less. All he could think about was Kate.

With Valentine's Day barely two days away, Paul gathered up his courage and paid a visit to the compound drugstore, where he bought a blank card with a drawing of a red rose on the cover. He walked around with it in his book bag for better than a hour until he finally sat down on the curb, opened it, and hastily wrote inside: "I love you. If you feel the same, say yes." Then, before his courage fled, he hastily signed his name and dropped the card in the mailbox.

Valentine's Day came and went. Paul could barely sit in his seat. Meanwhile, Kate acted unaffected; she didn't so much as glance in his direction. Paul felt his stomach sink. By midafternoon a depression had settled over him, and he got into trouble again for fighting.

After school Paul wandered around and ruminated: had he really signed the card? Had he gotten the address right? Could it possibly have gotten lost? Had he forgotten the stamp? He cursed himself for not having the nerve to write down a return address.

In early May, Paul was returning home from school one afternoon, taking his usual route across a vast and treeless expanse of closely cut grass, when out of the corner of his eye he spotted a figure walking toward him. At a distance the image shimmered in the heat, and all he could make out was the outline of a dress and a face framed in blond hair. Then, with a start, he realized it was Kate. His heart immediately started to pound in his chest. He didn't think she'd seen him yet, and he quickly glanced around, looking for a means of escape. But of course there was none—only open field all around. Then the thought occurred to Paul that it would look incredibly stupid to change direction suddenly. So he kept going, swallowing hard.

They drew closer. As she emerged from the shimmering heat, the girl's features became clearer. It was Kate, allright—in a white flowered dress, with hair braided and curled around her head. Paul's heart beat faster and faster. His mind raced. Had she recognized him? Would he dare to look at her as they passed?

The final twenty yards seemed endless. Paul had unconsciously quickened his pace. It would be like cars passing on a highway. Then, just as they were no more than six or seven feet apart—about to pass, seemingly into eternity—Kate looked up and over, directly into Paul's eyes. She smiled into his frozen face. "Yes," she said, and walked on.

A year later Paul and his twin brother were sent off to the United States for private preparatory schooling. Paul still did not like school much, but he had pretty much resigned himself to doing the work. His fighting days were largely behind him as well. He and his brother both went to good colleges; from there his brother went on to a highly rated business school, while Paul became a lawyer and ended up on the legal fast track. He started drinking during his prep school years and continued right through college. By the time he was in law school, Paul was an alcoholic. Looking back he did not know how he got through, being drunk most of the time. Similarly, he did not know how he had managed to be so successful at law.

It was after his third arrest for driving while intoxicated that

Paul's drinking problem finally caught up with him. The judge gave him the option of jail (which at that time and in that state could have jeopardized his career) or treatment. Paul signed himself into a rehabilitation center, got sober, and started going to AA meetings, which he continued to do for ten years thereafter. At the time I met him, he had not had a drink in more than twelve years.

Paul met his wife, Jennifer, at a conference where he was an invited speaker. He had been sober for about four years by then; their romance was quick and intense, and within three months they were married. Jennifer said that she had been attracted to a certain sensitivity, vulnerability, and gentleness she perceived in Paul. She decided to trust this perception over her initial impression that he was arrogant and self-centered. Paul was also bright and could be very funny. Moreover, unlike many of the men she had dated, Paul did not appear to be put off by her intellect or ambition.

One thing that did make Jennifer uncomfortable, though (aside from his sporadic bursts of arrogance), was a tendency Paul had to become sullen at times for no apparent reason. Also, despite his success in the competitive legal arena, Paul manifested a distinct dislike for conflict in his private life. Whenever an issue arose between he and Jennifer, no matter how minor, Paul would withdraw, stubbornly refusing to communicate. Coupled with his willingness to concede too easily in an argument, Jennifer found this part of Paul's personality exasperating. In her mind, though, having to put up with these quirks was a small price to pay for what she otherwise considered a first-rate marriage.

Jennifer noticed a definite change in Paul after their first child, a son, was born. The baby was born prematurely and developed some medical complications that required considerable attention, and so the decision was made that Jennifer would stay home longer than had first been planned. The couple's sex life until then had been very active, with Paul desiring it almost daily, but now it slowed down. This was partly because Jenny found herself more tired, but also, she thought, because Paul seemed to react so strongly whenever she would turn him down. It was like when they argued; he would become sullen and moody, sometimes for days. She found this had a negative effect on her own sex drive.

On the one hand, Jennifer felt bad for Paul, and not a little guilty. On the other hand, she resented his lack of understanding that caring for a sickly child was a stressful and tiring occupation, and that being home all day was also stressful because she was not used to it. Moreover, she did not feel as attractive as she had before she got pregnant. As a result of all this, Jennifer just was not as interested in sex as she had been.

Their son was about two, and Jennifer was pregnant again, when Paul began to talk about his desire to have an affair. He told her that he found himself "obsessing" about other women. This was not entirely new, he added, explaining that he had been having sexual fantasies about other women for as long as he could remember. He had never actually had an affair, he said, but he thought about it a lot. Jennifer was upset, but she decided not to pursue the issue further other than to make it clear to Paul that she would absolutely not tolerate, much less condone, any infidelity on his part.

Things came crashing down around Paul (and consequently Jennifer's) ears about six months later. Paul came home early one day, sat down heavily, and without looking up told Jenny that he had been forced to resign from his job. Why? Two separate sexual harassment complaints had been filed by women who worked for him. It seemed that he had been talking to one about his sexual frustrations at home, and had asked the second if she had any single friends he might date. The partners of the firm had held a hasty meeting, called Paul in, and handed him a check for a month's salary. If he did not accept it and submit his resignation on the spot, they said, they would fire him.

Against the advice of her friends to cut her losses and divorce Paul immediately, Jennifer decided to stay and see if the issues that were responsible for Paul's apparent professional suicide could be resolved. Despite her anger, she told me, and in spite of the tension between them over sex, she believed in her heart that Paul could be a loving husband and a devoted father. She was comfortable with his being a recovering alcoholic, but she knew nothing about sex addiction and feared it. Still, she decided to follow through, at least for a while, on her belief in Paul's potential.

William was born in Manchester, Vermont, a small town in the shadow of mountains that were later to become a vacation mecca for affluent city dwellers. Back then the hillsides were not yet scarred by fifty-yard-wide ski trails, and life was certainly quieter, if not quite as simple and serene as nostalgia might tempt us to believe. Old-timers say, though, that the winter snow was definitely deeper then, and that from mid-October right through April the air in the valleys was heavy with the smell of burning wood. The stores in town saw more business from locals than from out-of-towners, and they sold as much raw fabric as finished clothing. There were only a couple of restaurants, and the number of people who farmed was far greater than it is today. People traveled a lot less, and a big trip meant a daylong trek to Wilmington and back. It was a time and place where families were at least physically close, where the institution of marriage was just starting to change, and where divorce would still make a boy like William different from his peers.

William was just ten when his father abandoned the family for parts unknown. The memory of his leaving, without so much as a word of good-bye, remained etched in William's memory all his life. William, his mother, and his younger sister moved in with his maternal grandparents. His mother got a divorce and, not long after, told her son that he and his sister would be staying on while she moved to Boston to study medicine.

How did William cope with these separations, which came so closely one after the other? Judging by outside appearances, he did fine. He succeeded in school and demonstrated from an early age an exceptional talent for inventiveness and a capacity for perseverance. His grandparents provided for his physical needs, and his relationship with his grandfather (a steady, though usually quiet man) was not without its good moments. William impressed the old man as being a quick study. On one occasion, for example, William was writing a report for school on Australia. The old man casually commented on how only that country's aborigines knew the secret of constructing a good boomerang. Six months later William invited his grandfather to come outside to demonstrate the airworthiness of his latest creation—a homemade boomerang.

Secretly, of course, William felt the loss of his parents keenly. It was only much later, as an adult, that he dared to share his secret belief that he had caused their divorce. In his child's mind, both his father's and his mother's leaving made sense only as reflections of his own unlovability. The abandonment rendered him more or less permanently distrustful; its legacy was a craving for love that he tried to fulfill with substitutes, including money, attention, drugs, and alcohol.

The willingness to rise to a challenge that manifested itself so early in William's character evolved into an ambition that today would be called driven. He abandoned Vermont for New York, where he was initially a successful (though bored) law student and eventually made it big as a broker. His drive was always marked, however, by recklessness that led him to place his success at risk. Also, he liked to drink. Looking back on this life-style, William would have this to say about those years in New York: "Wall Street had me in its grip. Business and financial leaders were my heroes. Out of an alloy of drink and speculation, I forged the weapon that one day would turn in its flight like a boomerang and all but cut me to ribbons."[15]

Even after his recovery from alcoholism, William continued his pattern of working to excess. Though his own marriage survived where that of his parents had not, he seemed almost phobic regarding family life, preferring the less intimate role of organizer and builder. William (better known to the world as Bill Wilson) became a prolific writer and correspondent, and the organization he helped to build—Alcoholics Anonymous—continues to grow to this day.

Michael, barely seventeen, had already spent the better part of four years—nearly a quarter of his life—in correctional institutions like the one he was in when I first met him. He was stretched out on a thin three-by-six foot mattress on the floor of a six-by-ten cell, naked except for a pair of jockey shorts. His dark skin glistened with sweat. The bed that was supposed to go with the mattress, a steel frame strung with sagging wire and springs, stood off in one corner. There was no other furniture in the tiny space.

Three of the cell walls were made of concrete blocks; the fourth was barred. The walls had all been painted in a glossy off-white enamel that long ago had turned an ugly off-yellow. Innumerable names and initials were carved into them, along with dates that bore witness to the age of the facility. At the back, so high up that one could not see out of it, was a narrow window. It was fogged with dust and covered by a heavy latticework of flat steel strips that also had once been white but were now brown with accumulated grime. The window, which had long since lost its ability to be cranked open from within, bathed the cell in a diffuse gray light. A fan at one end of the long corridor produced more noise than breeze. The lights had been turned off in an effort to minimize heat production, and perhaps to give an illusion of coolness. Outside it was eighty degrees; inside it must have been at least ninety. The whole place smelled of sweat.

Michael's was one of twenty cells, ten on each side of a long corridor. At one end was the guard station. Two thin white women in their twenties and a heavyset black man with thinning hair were on duty. They spent nearly all of their time in the station, out of sight of their wards but with the door to the corridor propped open. As I stood among them a table fan, set atop an empty desk across the room, swiveled back and forth, throwing out weak waves of air that I soon learned to correlate my breathing with.

It was getting close to lunchtime, one of the guards casually remarked, apparently to explain why "the kids" were getting louder. Indeed, it struck me that with each passing minute the din outside the open doorway grew louder and more intense. If I listened more closely I could make out, through the cacophony of sounds, racial and sexual slurs, wolf howls, taunts, and angry curses. Take away the language, I thought, and it sounded very much like a kennel at feeding time. The doors of the cells were made of the same heavy steel lattice as the window covering. For some reason, they had been recently painted a bright, irritating green. Looking at them made me think of those portable cages that people use to transport their pets.

By pressing their faces up close up to the bars, the occupants within could see perhaps two-thirds the length of the hallway. They were all there, I knew, because they had committed crimes serious enough to earn them the classification of serious juvenile offenders—SJOs, for short. Their crimes ranged from murder to armed robbery to assault with a deadly weapon. The staff referred to them simply as "the heavy hitters." Of the twenty, only one was white. I was told that they were let out one at a time for forty-five minutes a day for "school," which meant meeting with a teacher and laboring through a page in a workbook on basic reading or math. The rest of the time they either slept, read old magazines, wrote letters, or took turns watching a television that was periodically moved to different places in the corridor. Moving the television was often the only reason the guards left their station.

Michael, I learned to my amazement, was a prolific letter writer. His caseworker explained to me that she encouraged him to write. A form of therapy, she called it. Therapy? I thought. I asked who he wrote to. Mostly to his friends on the outside, the caseworker replied, and sometimes to his mother.

In time I got to know Michael well. I discovered that in addition to his capacity for impulsive violence, his proclivity for stealing, and his involvement in drug dealing, he was a very bright, occasionally funny, and grossly undereducated youth. For him, however, school had about as much relevance (and appeal) as learning to milk cows. He was the product of one of Connecticut's many inner-city housing projects. A state with one of the nation's highest per capita incomes, Connecticut is also home to several of its poorest cities and some of its highest urban crime rates. On the streets of the neighborhood that Michael called home I had seen boys who had been shot in the face—innocent bystanders in the ongoing drug wars—and young girls with pregnant bellies and needle-scarred arms.

In the course of one of our talks Michael told me he was the father of two children, a boy and a girl, by different girlfriends. He explained to me that the girls he knew where not ignorant of birth control. On the contrary, he said, they were willing mothers. His current girlfriend, whom he had not seen in several months, was living with her grandmother, along with his ten-month-old daughter. He expected her to be completely faithful to him while he was doing his time; she had done time in this very same institution, though she and Michael had not known each other there. Michael's first girlfriend, along with his son, had moved to Florida, and he had not heard anything about her in over a year.

When he was not in one institution or another, Michael spent his time on the street, where he worked selling drugs. Many of his customers were adults and teens from out of town. He explained to me that he never tried to cheat them (for example, by selling them bad stuff) and that as a result of this sound business practice he had a substantial number of regular customers. He was completely loyal to his mother—a sometimes recovering alcoholic and cocaine addict—and his younger brother and sister. He slept at home whenever he was not sleeping with his girlfriend. Michael helped his mother out by giving her some of the money he earned by selling drugs, and also by scaring off any men he suspected of wanting to use her for sex or money. Michael's mom took care of the apartment, cooked meals and washed clothes, and worked part-time at a local supermarket. She never asked Michael where he got the money he gave her.

In seventeen years, Michael had seen his father exactly twice. The first time was when the man had shown up unannounced in the middle of the night and began making uninvited sexual advances toward Michael's mother. Michael was five or six at the time, and the man's intimidating manner scared him. He did not realize that his father was high on drugs, or that he was carrying a gun. He just blindly went after this man who had helped conceive him, pummeling him with both fists in an effort to protect his mother. He remembered hearing his father laughing, then saying something to his mother before he pried Michael away, threw him to the floor, turned, and left. Michael recalled his mother crying afterward as the sound of footfalls in the hallway grew fainter.

The second and last time Michael saw his father was when someone else pointed him out; otherwise Michael would never have known who it was. He was walking toward Michael, but on the other side of the street. He was dressed in a shiny dark suit set off by a gleaming white shirt and a bright red tie. His shoes were patent leather and glittered even from a distance. Michael knew the look— that of a drug dealer. He watched the man pass; their eyes never met. A year later Michael heard that his father had been shot dead in New York City. He could not recall having a reaction.

Whenever our eyes met, Michael's distrust was palpable. In his world he was respected on account of his reputation for toughness and persistence. If you crossed Michael, sooner or later you would pay the price. Even within the confines of an institution populated by tough young men, no one challenged him lightly. In groups, I noticed, he would occasionally be confronted by a counselor and challenged to express his thoughts and feelings on some matter. Michael would immediately turn sullen. If some foolish group member dared to support this confrontation, that young person had better be ready to fight later on. Michael was the toughest in a world of tough young men, and beneath his soft, round, dark eyes there lurked a coldness that sometimes made me shiver. He told me matter-of-factly that he smoked pot daily, and that sometimes he used cocaine. But he was adamant that he did not have a "drug problem." Asked what his goals were, he replied unapologetically that he intended to become a "high roller"—someone who got rich selling drugs. He was already on his way and had plans to buy his first BMW just as soon as he could get his license, which had been put off on account of his having to do more time.

Tom and Sally sat on opposite sides of the couch. Though I had seen each of them at different times during the past three years, especially Tom, I had not seen either of them for quite a while. The last I knew they were living together, and Tom had told me they were hoping to buy a house and get married. Then I got Tom's call and heard the urgency and tension in his voice. "Things are not going very well," he had said in his usual self-controlled manner. I took that to mean that things were actually terrible and asked him how soon they wanted to meet. "As soon as possible," he replied.

Tom was one of those men with a drinking problem who is able to stay sober for about six months at a time. His "mini-slips" would vary both in duration and intensity; at worst, he would stay drunk for a week and miss a day or two of work. This had been the pattern for the past several years. Before that were times when he had been drunk literally for months at a time, lost jobs, and run himself deeply in debt by buying all sorts of things that caught his fancy. Over my two years of work with Tom there were three minor slips but no major relapses, and he had worked his way out from under a virtual mountain of debt.

Sally was ten years younger than Tom and, unlike him, had neither been married nor had a drinking problem. Long ago, when I had asked Sally what she liked about Tom, she said it was the air of determination he gave off. "When I'm with Tom I feel that I'm with a man who knows what he wants. He can be a lot of fun, but he's also serious. The men my own age I've dated don't seem to know what they want at all, including whether they want a relationship." Now, two years later, Tom's seriousness had turned out to be a mixed blessing for Sally.

As they settled into the couch I could see the tension in their faces. I was used to knowing Tom as an individual with a friendly but determined (if not somewhat overbearing) manner; the expression on Sally's face, however, was new to me. In our few previous meetings she had consistently come across as an intelligent and exceptionally friendly young woman, and one who also was accommodating. For example, she expressed her tolerance of Tom's biannual mini-slips so cheerfully it made me slightly uncomfortable. At one point I asked her if she felt she might be minimizing the extent of Tom's problem. After all, he had only recently paid off thousands of dollars of debt he had incurred during his several relapses.

"I know what you're saying," Sally explained, "and I do think about that sometimes. But for the two years I've known Tom he's never slipped for more than a week. It's never been anything like the slips—relapses, I'd guess, is a better word—that he used to have. If that happens, I suppose it could be a big problem. I'd have to think about what I would want to do."

Now I perceived a seriousness in Sally's expression that made me realize that this was a woman who, despite her youth and her tolerance, clearly had a mind and spirit of her own. I wondered how Tom was dealing with this. Not too well, I discovered.

"So, what's up?" I asked.

Tom leaned forward to speak, but he was cut off by Sally. "I feel as though we don't have any relationship at all any more," she said. "I feel as though all we are is some kind of partnership—a business arrangement. All we talk about now is money. We never go out. We never talk about anything else. I feel like Tom scrutinizes every thing I do, and I feel guilty every time I spend a dollar. My whole paycheck goes into the household account, while his goes into his account. Then I'm made to feel guilty every time I withdraw ten dollars from the ATM."

"Why do you think that's happened?" I asked.

Sally glared at Tom, and he looked away. "The damned house!" Sally exclaimed. "Ever since he decided we—I mean *he*—had to get a house, he's been obsessed with it. And our life together has gone down the tubes. We're not even married yet, and already I feel like a burned-out wife!"

Tom acknowledged that he was "preoccupied" with buying a house. His defense was that Sally had agreed that buying a house was a good idea. When she responded by saying that she no longer wanted to buy a house unless their relationship got better, Tom replied that it was his intention to make an offer on a house and apply for a mortgage within the next sixty days, with or without her.

This remark infuriated Sally all the more, and she responded by pulling out the stops. "So it doesn't really matter what I want, is that it, Tom? I have two choices, as usual: your way, or no way. Well, what if my choice is no way?"

At this point I intervened to try to prevent one or both of them from saying anything they might regret. But I also felt that Tom needed to hear Sally out, as well as to reconsider whether he really wanted to issue the kind of ultimatum he just had. Once things had cooled down sufficiently, I asked Sally to explain to me why she seemed so angry. Was it just the house and Tom's preoccupation with managing money?

"I just feel like he wants me under his thumb," she replied. I don't feel that he trusts me to make decisions, or to be responsible. I feel like I'm a teenager and he's my father. He doesn't even like me to see my friends. You should hear how he talks to them! Not one of them is willing to visit me at our place now, because they're afraid of Tom! Whenever I go out he wants to know where I'm going, who I'll be with, and exactly when I'll be back. It drives me crazy!"

"But you won't tell me where you're going!" Tom protested, "And you're usually back late these days. Don't you think I have a right to know where you are? Remember, I've worked in bars, and I know the kinds of things that can go on there."

Sally shot back with a proverbial look that could kill.

As I listened to Tom defend himself I could not help but feel a little sorry for him, even as I sensed that Sally was telling the truth. I had come to know that she could be very insecure herself, and that she also had a tendency to avoid dealing with issues and facing up to responsibilities that could get her into hot water at times. Still, Tom was not only an alcoholic struggling with recovery, but also a work-aholic and a man who was obsessed with controlling everything from money to his girlfriend's relationships. He employed an arsenal of defenses to persuade Sally (and perhaps himself as well) that this wasn't so. The facts spoke for themselves, however, including Tom's admission that he was preoccupied with finances, obsessed with buying a house, and in danger of burning out as a result of too much work and too little play. His weekends, he acknowledged, had become nothing more than a long list of things to be done. They left him exhausted. "I've always been a list person," he explained. "I make lists of things to do, and once something gets on the list I don't feel right until it's done." I asked him how he felt when he did erase something from the list. "Relieved," he replied.

Tom rationalized his obsession with money and buying a house as something he wanted for both himself and Sally, yet he hedged when I casually asked when the two of them planned to get married. He saw that as something they would do at some vague point in time when they were, in his words, "settled." And in terms of controlling Sally's relationships, Tom confessed that he was a jealous man, adding patronizingly that Sally was young and attractive and one could not trust the men she might run into at a bar. When Sally responded that she only went to bars with friends, to socialize over no more than two drinks, Tom nodded. "I know that's what *you're* there for Sally," he said. "But I don't know what your friends are there for."

Last of all was Sally's complaint that Tom never talked to or listened to her. She confronted him with a number of examples of times when he had simply told her that he was not interested in hearing about what went on at her work. She was of the impression that he minimized her career struggles while becoming preoccupied with his own. At the same time, he refused to talk to her about his frustrations on the job but would spend considerable time discussing them over the phone with male friends and his AA sponsor. Tom's excuse that he did not want to burden Sally with these problems came across as facile, and she threw it off with a wave of her hand.

Clearly Tom and Sally had some work to do if their relationship was to move away from the addictive quality that Tom seemed bent on bringing to it, toward the intimacy and mutuality that she was looking for and that, in truth, I thought he could benefit from as well. Tom and Sally later separated, and Tom had to wait nearly two years to buy the house he so desperately wanted. Yet in the end it turned out, in his words, to be the best disappointment in his life.

On the surface these men are vastly different from one another, whether we measure that difference in terms of age or circumstance, yet underneath they have much in common. To begin with, they are all addicts. Paul's sex addiction persisted even as he recovered from alcoholism. Bill Wilson, of course, was an alcoholic, though he also experimented with other drugs and by contemporary standards might even be called a workaholic.[16] Michael was clearly addicted to marijuana, but also in my opinion to power and money. He liked the high, for example, that having a wad of money in his pocket gave him, as well as the high he got from having others defer to him. Tom, finally, was still struggling to control his use of alcohol and was more or less out of control of his own preoccupation with sex and money.

All of these men had also developed a *tolerance:* they either needed to use more of their substances of choice to get high or found that engaging in their addictive behavior patterns brought them less of a kick over time. Tolerance drives the addict to "chase highs," meaning using more of something and becoming progressively more preoccupied with it. It also drives them to seek ever more powerful highs. The cocaine user will try crack, for example, and the pothead will forever be searching for a more powerful weed. Similarly, the workaholic will seek bigger and bigger challenges, the sex addict will seek out more exciting (and usually riskier) situations, and so on. All of these men did all of these things.

The addict continues to pursue his craving and his obsession regardless of negative consequences. The AA "Big Book" *(Alcoholics Anonymous)* is replete with alcoholics' tales of loss, as is other twelve-step fellowship literature. But this same pattern holds true for other addicts as well. Paul, for instance, continued to fantasize about and flirt with women, even after losing his job and nearly losing his marriage. Tom continued to behave in the ways that Sally described long after she had warned him, leaving her no self-respecting choice other than to leave. And I fear to think what awaited Michael once he left the institution.

Every addict I have ever spoken to has been able to relate to me the feeling of excitement, and in some cases relief, he or she felt at the first occurrence of a behavior that later became an addiction. For Bill Wilson this feeling was associated with being in a tavern, drinking, and being aware of a sense of comradeship and a feeling of belonging[17]—something he apparently was not accustomed to.

Interestingly enough it was very much this same sort of feeling that Paul sought through falling in love with women. Rather than seeking the comfort of men's company, however, he became obsessed with his fantasy of romantic love. The high he felt that day when he passed Kate on the field and she said "yes" was a feeling he never forgot. It was, I suspected, the response he'd always sought from his parents. He spent much time and energy, and also risked a great deal, in its pursuit. When I asked him to describe the feeling it gave him, the words he chose were *connected* and *secure.*

Naturally Michael related to this idea when I asked him about feeling high. At first I thought it might be danger to which he was addicted. As it turned out, though, he used as much marijuana as he did in order to get some relief from the tension he felt at having to live a dangerous life. He got high not on danger, but primarily on being top dog—on being tough and on having money. The fact that most young men in his situation rarely lived to see their twenty-first birthday was a thought he kept hidden behind a haze of marijuana.

When I asked Tom the same question about feeling high, he had several responses. First, he said, he recalled the first time he had a drink. He was about twelve. "It's funny you should ask, but I can still recall the feeling of *mellowness* that came over me when I drank. I believe I still drink for that same reason."

Tom also told me that from the time he was a child he could experience what he likened to a chemically induced high in other ways. For example, he reported feeling high after making a list of things to do and then doing them all. This was different, he explained, than any simple feeling of satisfaction; it was an "intoxicating" experience. Of course he could get also a high, he said, from spending money (something I could relate to). Finally, if he was trying to resist the urge to spend, he could try to "squeeze a high," as he put it, out of pinching pennies and denying himself.

Psychologically, all of the these men were motivated in large part by a rigid adherence to a positional or hierarchical view of themselves in relation to others. Their self-esteem was founded primarily on seeing themselves in contrast to others, and their social orientation focused heavily on differences and on assessing relative position. Power, control, and social status were some of the key dimensions of difference by which they were (largely unconsciously) driven. This orientation to self and others has decided psychological effects; it renders the individual more or less chronically *insecure,* since more preoccupation with maintaining one's relative position inevitably occurs. Some personal factors that seem to mediate just how preoccupied a man will become with maintaining his relative position are discussed later.

A second consequence of a rigidly positional perspective on self and others is chronic *isolation*. Being concerned with differences and relative position, men become limited in their capacity to identify with one another. At times, depending upon their personal histories, they strongly resist such identification. This renders them vulnerable to isolation and loneliness.

The two central dynamics of addiction, then—insecurity and isolation—are illustrated by these four stories. What all addictions have in common is that they represent efforts to compensate for tenuous self-esteem and to comfort oneself in the face of chronic isolation and loneliness. Unless these personal issues are addressed, a man will continue to carry this vulnerability to new addictions within him, even as he "recovers" from one or more of them.

In the next chapter I will examine some of the historical roots of men's predisposition toward a positional orientation. This will be important for two reasons. First, it will help to put the issue in perspective. It is altogether too easy, I think, to make false assumptions about the "nature" of men and women in the absence of a social-historical context. Just as historical biographers can commit the error of *"presentism"*[17] (the tendency to assume that historical figures were driven by thoughts and feelings similar to those of modern men and women), it seems easy for psychotherapists to assume that the men and women they see in their offices think, feel, and act the same as men and women always have.

The second area in which a historical perspective will be helpful is in developing ideas for what men can do in order to reduce their vulnerability to addiction. It is one thing to say that men suffer from insecurity and isolation; it is quite another to offer something useful regarding what they can do about it.

2

Masculinity Revisited

To understand men, it is important first of all to appreciate that they view the social world in terms of relative position. Men orient themselves in social situations with the help of cognitive hierarchies; placed in an unstructured situation, the first thing they are apt to do is to structure it cognitively in a hierarchical fashion. Implicit in this process is placing oneself somewhere within that hierarchy. As a consequence of this tendency virtually all of men's relationships, from their most competitive to their most intimate, are colored to some degree by perceptions of differences and differentials.

At the bottom line it is power or status, as measured in one way or another, that forms the basis for men's self-esteem and their orientation of themselves in relation to others. In contrast, women are disposed to view the social world relationally (that is, in terms of who is close to whom) and to define and measure themselves much more by the quality of their relationships than by how much relative power or status they have. Although these gender differences appear to be in a state of flux, this difference in orientation appears largely valid. A central question, however, is whether this difference between men and women, and specifically men's positional orientation, reflects "the way men are" in a biological sense, or whether it represents the effects of socialization. To answer this we need a historical perspective on gender differences and sex roles.

Most of the influential books on the psychology of men and women that appeared as the profession of psychotherapy emerged at the beginning of this century were written by men, and their focus with respect to problems of male-female relationships could be said to have been "the problem with women." Women were thought to be difficult, as Freud's supposed comment—"What do women want?"—implied. Along with many other men, Freud concluded that the root of women's difficultness lay in the reality of their penislessness:[19] it was simple envy, amplified perhaps by anger and resentment, that drove women to drive men crazy. From the male viewpoint of these authors, a positional orientation (along with its behavioral correlates such as competitiveness) was assumed to be healthy. Conversely, one can infer that a relational orientation made them uncomfortable, for it was this perspective that they pathologized. Thus, dependency became an illness, separation became the goal of development, and autonomy emerged as the epitome of mental health.

From the psychoanalytic perspective, even father-son competition (as represented in the Oedipal complex) was thought to be normal and healthy, and only those males who were unsuccessful at resolving this conflict and orienting themselves relative to their fathers in some positional (one up–one down) manner were thought to suffer from such pathologies as homosexuality and depression. To some extent Wilhelm Reich, especially in his discussion of the phallic-narcissistic personality,[20] and also Alfred Adler in his discussions of overcompensation and striving for superiority,[21] perceived the dangers inherent in an excessive concern with position and its resulting obsession with power and control. Of the major early personality and psychotherapy theorists, however, only Adler, through his concept of social interest,[22] sought to lay out solutions in a domain that could even loosely be called relational. Interestingly enough, although these early psychoanalysts and neoanalysts offered up their theories as generic, in perspective it seems that they were primarily talking about men. The *intrapersonal* (as opposed to interpersonal) focus is decidedly masculine, as is their model of mental health.

Now, at the other end of the century, we see books being written by women, who in turn are having their say about relationships. Is it a coincidence, then, that we find ourselves confronted with a plethora of theories that fundamentally pathologize men? Is it any wonder that we now have books explaining that men fundamentally hate women?[23] Or books asserting that many women's main problem lies in their insistence on loving dysfunctional men who mistreat and misunderstand them?[24]

We have been told recently that men strive to dominate and control women as a revenge of sorts for having been dominated and controlled by them through infancy and childhood.[25] We have been told that men are afraid of intimacy with women on account of having, as boys, to separate from (and presumably "reject") their mothers.[26] No doubt other theories will appear, presenting even more women's views of "the problem with men."

As a man, I feel that none of these theories squares with my perceptions of reality, probably for the same reason that men's theories of female personality development seem foreign to most women. None of the men I described in the first chapter, for instance, struck me as having rejected their mothers. I think I could make the case, though, that some had been rejected by their mothers, their fathers, or both. The emphasis in these writings on the singular importance of the mother-son relationship in male personality development and men's subsequent problems in relationships may represent little more than the female equivalent of the sort of thinking that dominated early psychoanalysis, which was unduly preoccupied with girls' presumed envy of and sexual attraction toward their fathers. These theories seek to reduce problems of adult men and women to dysfunctional early relationships with their parents. At best this may be naive; at worst it is a distraction that draws men and women to focus their time and energy on a past that cannot be changed while giving them little direction for improving their *adult* relationships. For men in particular, this approach represents a blind alley when it comes to offering solutions that they can pursue if they want to build self-esteem, open themselves to intimacy, and reduce their vulnerability to addiction.

Still, the question is a valid one: what *is* the problem with men? Why is it that so many men today feel confused about their relationships with women, so fearful of opening up, and so isolated from other men? Why do so many of them tell me that they are struggling with their identities as men? Why is it that so many of them experience near-panic reactions when they are confronted by intimacy? Why are they so insecure, so inclined to take the defensive and to try to control their relationships? Why, finally, are they so much more vulnerable than women to becoming addicts? To cast some light on questions like these, we need to step back for a moment and take a look from the perspective of history at relationships and at the way we have come to define masculinity and femininity.

We live in a time when our traditional concepts of masculinity and femininity are being challenged by a new social archetype, as presented in the concept of *androgyny*.[27] For reasons that may become clearer through this historical review, it was adaptive in the past for men and women to be socialized to follow two different and largely complementary developmental paths associated with social archetypes that over time became defined as masculinity and femininity. These archetypes are reflected in differences not only in dress and appearance but, more importantly, in behavior, attitudes, and orientation toward self and others—in short, in personality.

There is reason to believe that the trend toward complementary socialization began in earnest early in the nineteenth century. Certainly by the middle of that century it was a dominant trend in society, with men and women being channeled into dramatically different and largely complementary roles. Before then relationships were different; in eighteenth-century America, for example, the rate of premarital intercourse, and therefore also of premarital pregnancy, was relatively high. Even in the early nineteenth century nearly one-third of New England brides, many of whom were still in their teens, were already pregnant.[28] Obviously, premarital sex was more the rule than the exception. Among other things this meant that for the majority of couples family life coincided fairly closely with married life. Family life revolved around the themes of shared work, child rearing, and collective survival. What we now think of as sex roles were largely defined by work responsibilities, but they were not nearly so sharply defined as they were to become. Despite some differences there was a great deal of collaborative work, as well as interchangeability between men and women, or mothers and fathers.

The nineteenth century witnessed the emergence of two social events or processes that may well have been the driving forces behind the divergence of men and women and the emergence of the masculine and feminine social archetypes. The first process was the steady growth of industrialization, and the second was the emergence of the middle class.

As the nineteenth century progressed, and as industrialization led to the growth of cities and a more stratified society, values and roles changed; men, women, and relationships changed with them. One new trend was toward sexual restraint and family planning, with women being the ones who were expected to be virtuous and to set limits. This resulted, among other things, in the premarital pregnancy rate dropping precipitously (from one in three to one in five or six) by the 1840s.[29] By the 1830s, a rushed marriage in the middle class was considered in some circles to be "a case of seduction,"[30] with the woman bearing the brunt of the shame.

It was in the context of this kind of social change that new male and female roles, along with new definitions of masculinity and femininity, emerged. Key to these new concepts was the progressive channeling of women and men into the emotional-relational and vocational-instrumental domains of life, respectively. Women (especially middle-class women) were increasingly expected to devote themselves to home and children, whereas men were encouraged to establish themselves in the world of work and to provide for the family's financial needs. As a consequence, women were encouraged to develop personal qualities compatible with the responsibilities of caring for others. Men, on the other hand, were encouraged to develop qualities that would serve them well at work. Over time, I suggest, this social trend led to the divergence of men and women toward positional versus relational orientations toward self and others.

Today we increasingly expect men and women to be both nurturers and providers—in a word, to be androgynous. Since at least the nineteenth century, relationships have been founded more on complementarity (the idea of "two making one"). Rather than being interchangeable, sex roles have become increasingly complementary and specialized over time. This may have made relationships and families more efficient at one time, and presumably it met the demands of social adaptation, but psychologically it also led to a trend of socially enforced alienation between the sexes. By the middle of the nineteenth century this division was so noticeably a part of American society that the visiting Alexis de Tocqueville was moved to comment on the myriad ways in which American men and women were encouraged "to follow paths that [were] always different."[31]

As part of the emerging sex roles that defined men and women as different and complementary, men and masculinity were associated with strength, emotional restraint, endurance, toughness, and reason. Women and femininity, in contrast, were associated with feeling and sensitivity, with nurturance and intuition. As Ralph Waldo Emerson expressed it, "Man's sphere is out of doors and among men—woman's is in the house—Man seeks for power and influence—woman for order and beauty—Man is just—woman is kind."[32] This thinking about the nature of men and women was not limited to the likes of Emerson. It was common thinking, as the following, written by John Patch, an editor, in 1848, reveals:

> Where courage, activity and endurance are required, there is the place for man—where cleanliness, order, affection and all the finer sensibilities of the heart and soul are needed for comfort and consolation in the difficulties and trials of life, there should bloom the never fading rose of woman's constancy and affection.[33]

Nineteenth-century men were encouraged to build self-esteem on personal qualities such as strength, endurance, self-control, and competence in the world. They were not expected to be especially pure in thought or deed, since it was assumed that the world was too rough a place for the angelic. Instead, it became the responsibility of women to live the moral life.[34] Clearly this social context and these expectations drove men increasingly toward a positional orientation regarding themselves and others. The ideal man was someone who was powerful, in control (of himself and of situations), and emotionally restrained.

This ideal of masculinity was romanticized in the novels of the time. In *Jane Eyre,* for example, the reserved Mr. Rochester speaks the words below at the very height of his most romantic, intense, and fateful encounter with Jane. Although he is so obviously and painfully in love with her, one can virtually feel the self-restraint in these lines:

> I sometimes have a queer feeling with regard to you— especially when you are near to me, as now: it is as if I had a string somewhere underneath my left ribs, tightly and inextricably knotted to a similar string situated in the corresponding quarter of your little frame.[35]

Now contrast this to the way that Jane speaks to him just slightly later:

> Do you think I can stay to become nothing to you? Do you think I am an automaton?—a machine without feelings?—and can bear to have

my morsel of bread snatched from my lips, and my drop of living water dashed from my cup? Do you think, because I am poor, obscure, plain, and little, I am soulless and heartless? You think wrong!—I have as much soul as you—and full as much heart! . . . It is my spirit that addresses your spirit; just as if both had passed through the grave, and we stood at God's feet, equals—as we are![36]

There is little doubt in my mind that at this point in history men were already beginning to be intimidated by women's emotionality, and to experience anxiety when faced with the prospect of having to meet women as equals on an emotional plane. I can almost see Mr. Rochester squirm in his seat at having to articulate his feelings and communicate them to Jane!

The male role that emerged in the nineteenth century—and that has shaped men's thinking about themselves and their relationships through the twentieth century—is no longer functional. It simply does not fit well with the realities of contemporary life, which is based no longer on complementarity but increasingly on the idea of interchangeability. Contemporary social trends that began in the post–World War I era include the mass exodus of women out of the home and into the workplace, the emergence of the dual-career family and the latchkey child, and the creation of suburbia. Ironically, although androgyny demands that men learn to be nurturant and relationally oriented, I believe we have seen much more change so far in the other direction: women learning to be competitive, emotionally self-controlled, and "in the world." In some ways, therefore, "the problem with men" and "the problem with women" have begun to converge. Men and women alike are experiencing the stresses inherent in an age when sex-role expectations, and consequently men's and women's very identities and orientations toward others, are in a state of flux.

The social archetype of masculinity that lingers on to this day owes its origins, I believe, not so much to biology as to a social context marked by rapid industrialization and the emergence of an economic middle class. These were the dominant social themes of the nineteenth century; they reached their zenith, however, in the Victorian era. This was the time when society made a quantum leap from industrialization toward an increasing preoccupation with consumption and acquisition, where advertising and marketing began to exert powerful influences over life-styles and desires, and where personal worth began to be measured more and more in terms of possessions and position.[37] This effectively increased the sex-role gap. Victorian middle-class women were encouraged to spend their time in the home and to devote themselves to mothering, homemaking, and maintaining the family's social connections. Whatever free time they had was apt to be spent in the company of other women. Men, meanwhile, spent more and more of their time pursuing credentials that would earn them (and their families) position and money.

In the Victorian era the divergence between men and women (and between masculine and feminine) extended itself to virtually every aspect of life. Eventually there were distinctly "masculine" versus "feminine" styles in virtually everything from clothing to furniture to art. This period of time was marked by popular images of men as strong and resilient, and of women as sensitive and delicate. Perhaps nowhere is this dichotomous thinking more evident than in Victorian books about sex, love, and relationships. Interestingly, popular writers of the time were wont to ascribe sex-role differences to nature much more than to any social forces driving men and women. Here is an example from one of the first "marriage manuals," a book written by Edward Carpenter in 1896 and romantically titled *Love's Coming-of-Age:*

> The sex passion in man is undoubtedly a force—huge and fateful—which has to be reckoned with. Perhaps (speaking broadly) all the passions and powers, the intellect and affections and emotions and all, are really profounder and vaster in Man than in Woman—are more varied, root deeper, and have wider scope; but then the woman has this advantage, that her powers are more co-ordinated, are in harmony with each other, where his are disjointed or in conflict.[38]

Only slightly later, Marie Stopes, another Victorian and one of the first "marriage doctors," had this to say about male and female sexuality in her even more widely read book, *Married Love:*

> "Now physical passion, so swiftly stimulated in a man, tends to override all else, and the untutored man seeks but one thing—the accomplishment of desire. . . . In our anemic artificial days it often happens that the man's desire is a surface need, quickly satisfied, colourless,

and lacking beauty, and that he has no knowledge of the rich complexities of lovemaking which an initiate of love's mysteries enjoys. To such a man his wife may indeed seem petulant, capricious, or resentful without reason.

Welling up in her are the wonderful tides, scented and enriched by the myriad experiences of the human race from its ancient days of leisure and flower-wreathed lovemaking, urging her to transports and to self-expressions.[39]

The Victorians extended their romantic notions of complementarity to their ideas about relationships and love. Edward Carpenter had this to say:

That there should exist one other person in the world towards whom all openness of interchange should establish itself, from whom there should be no concealment; whose body should be as dear to one, in every part, as one's own; with whom there should be no sense of Mine or Thine, in property or possession; into whose mind one's thoughts should naturally flow, as it were to know themselves and receive a new illumination; and between whom and oneself there should be a spontaneous rebound of sympathy in all the joys and sorrows and experiences in life; such is perhaps one of the dearest wishes of the soul.[40]

Stopes quoted Carpenter's text in *Married Love* and then went on to add her own thoughts on the matter of pairing:

Every heart desires a mate. For some reason beyond our comprehension, nature has so created us that we are incomplete in ourselves; neither man nor woman singly can know the joy of the performance of all the human functions; neither man nor woman singly can create another human being. This fact, which is expressed in our outward divergencies of form, influences and colours the whole of our lives; and there is nothing for which the innermost spirit of one and all so yearns as for a sense of union with another soul, and the perfecting of oneself which such union brings.[41]

Such descriptions of male and female sexuality and of relationships may seem humorous today, but they are totally consistent with popular social archetypes of masculinity and femininity that emerged in the nineteenth century and reached their most exaggerated forms in Victorian times. Moreover, these ideas have not died easily. Consider these excerpts from books about sex published in the 1960s:

> Men and women must understand the female anatomy before they appreciate woman's sexual response. Do you know why, for example, a woman responds much more to romancing, to soft talk and gentle caresses than a man does? It is because her sexual organs are largely concealed within the body, because her erotic zones are widely distributed over a large area of the body.
>
> A woman can be aroused to sexual climax when she is kissed, loved, made to feel wanted. But she must be gently wooed before her sexual desire makes itself known.
>
> A man, on the other hand, experiences a localized sexual feeling. His sex organs are outside the body where they can be stimulated in hundreds of ways every day. He is far more susceptible to erotic stimuli than a woman. And he often makes the mistake of thinking that she is experiencing the same sensations that he is—that she, too, is eager for immediate sexual gratification.[42]

> Much has been written about the need to "awaken" the woman sexually. Her sexual responsiveness, it has been said, is essentially a dormant quality, only a potential for arousal, until she begins her active sexual life. Such a statement has considerable truth in it. Many authors have pointed out the tragic consequences if the new husband does not use great caution in the early experiences of the marriage.[43]

The assumptions here are clear: man's sexuality is a powerful, driving force within him that is easily aroused and quickly satisfied; woman is sensitive and needs to be treated with care. Sex is also the man's responsibility, apparently, for he must "use great caution" lest there be "tragic consequences" for the sexual relationship.

Now, barely a generation after these words were written, many men and women would argue against these stereotypes of male and female sexuality and their implied stereotypes about masculinity and femininity. My point, however, is that the social archetypes underlying these views have a fairly long tradition behind them. It was not so very long ago that they were popular. Lastly, as a professional I must share my observation that many individuals and couples continue to struggle with issues such as whose responsibility it is to turn who on in bed, and how much "caressing" and "wooing" men and women respectively need. In any case, these associations of men and masculinity with power and control are entirely consistent with a positional orientation toward self and relationships, including sexual relationships. They are, in my view, at the root of the problem with men.

In the next chapter I will look even more closely at how Victorian social archetypes linger and how the sex-role divergence that began nearly two hundred years ago has affected the psychology of men, including their view of themselves and their approach to relationships. Based on that understanding I will begin to construct a map showing how men can escape the limitations imposed by a rigidly positional orientation.

3

Masculinity and Emotions

For the successful middle-class Victorian man, emotion and sensitivity had long ceased to be the currencies of relationships. Strength and self-restraint were qualities that lent themselves better than emotionality and sensitivity to survival in the increasingly competitive world of men, and they were accordingly idealized. Male heroes became increasingly big on strength, resilience, and determination, but short on sensitivity and communication. When men attempted to bring this "masculine" orientation into their relationships, what should have been expected? How do you feel and express tender love and sexual passion, for example, in a self-restrained or reserved way? How can you be vulnerable in a tough way? How deep can intimacy get if your emotional vocabulary is limited? How effective a team can you be if one person is preoccupied with being in control?

Victorian relationships were built on complementarity, an idea that was romanticized in the notions of opposites attracting and two becoming one. It did not seem to occur to most popular writers about relationships that this thinking represented a historical artifact, that it had not always been that way. But to the Victorians it made sense to think of love in terms of the attraction of opposites, and of marriage as the merging of two halves to form a whole. They assumed that this was nature at work.

The reality, I think, was that romantic Victorian notions of love and their emphasis on the complementarity of men and women reflected a gulf between the sexes that had already existed for several generations. It was evident in their divergent sex roles, and it was represented in their disparate orientations toward life. In contrast to men, and to complement them, women were encouraged to develop their emotional and communicative capacities—to be feeling and communicative beings—and to be nurturant, and sociable. As noted in Chapter 2, this has been labeled a relational orientation, in contrast to the positional orientation that is associated with being male. Of course one could argue that Victorian women were plenty concerned with position (meaning social position), as are many women today. Yet it is also true that women by this time in history were expected to carry the emotional and communicative burden in relationships. Men were expected to carry the financial burden.

The positional orientation to life is more conducive to contrast and comparison than to identification. When we take a positional orientation toward ourselves and others, we constantly measure everything from self-worth to success in relative terms. We are forever seeking to define our place on some hierarchy, from how much money we make to how many credentials we have to how good we are at something. We are driven constantly to seek out our turf and to defend it. As will be discussed further in the next chapter, this leads to a certain amount of chronic insecurity, as well a sense of isolation.

Beginning in the nineteenth century, a man's place was thought to be primarily out of the home, in the world, where over time competition increasingly reigned. In order to function effectively in this environment, men were socialized to be rugged and self-controlled. This social archetyping of men may in fact underlie most of the harsh socialization practices to which boys are subjected. We expose them to competition early to "toughen them up" and encourage them to jump into the fray. We chastise or ridicule them if they are not competitive enough, or if they show their emotional sensitivity too much. The systematic, culturally sanctioned neglect of boys' emotional sensitivities is a major story of abuse yet to be told. Men themselves conspire in this secrecy, thinking it unmanly to reveal their pain and tell their stories about what it is like to grow up male.

One consequence of the division of men and women into positional versus relational spheres of action was that women became more dependent on men for their material welfare, whereas men became dependent on women for their emotional welfare. Bronte's Jane Eyre and Flaubert's Emma Bovary, both nineteenth-century fictional characters, represent two archetypal examples of women whose emotional sensitivities defined their lives much more so than was the case for the men around them. The following excerpts are from Flaubert's novel *Madame Bovary:*

> In accordance with country custom, she offered him a drink. He declined. She pressed him. Finally she suggested with a laugh that they should take a liqueur together. She fetched a bottle of curacao from the cupboard, reached down two small glasses, filled one to the brim, poured the merest drop into the other and, after clinking glasses, raised hers to her lips. As there was practically nothing in it, she tilted her head right back to drink. With her head back and her lips rounded and the skin of her neck stretched tight, she laughed at her own vain efforts, and slid the tip of her tongue between her fine teeth to lick, drop by drop, the bottom of the glass.[44]

> She stood with her big flaming eyes fixed on him, with a serious, an almost terrible, look. Then they were dimmed with tears; her red eyelids lowered; she gave him her hands, and Leon was pressing them to his lips when a servant arrived to tell Monsieur that someone wanted him.[45]

Flaubert's Emma Bovary led an emotionally rich and sensual life. The men around her are colorless by comparison; even her lovers are no match for Emma's sensuality and passion. Interestingly, Flaubert himself once alluded to his envy of Emma, as well as hinting at something I have come to believe in—that men often live vicarious emotional lives. In describing his character once in an interview Flaubert remarked, "Madame Bovary, *c'est moi!*[46]

In D. H. Lawrence's *Lady Chatterley's Lover,* published nearly a century later, emotions still are expressed not primarily by men but by women:

> It was a night of sensual passion, in which she was a little startled and almost unwilling: yet pierced again with piercing thrills of sensuality, different, sharper, more terrible than the thrills of tenderness, but, at the moment, more desirable. Though a little frightened, she let him have his way, and the reckless, shameless sensuality shook her to her foundations, stripped her to the very last, and made a different woman of her.[47]

These fictional women led lives that were sensual and passionate. It was their feelings, as much as their ideas, that guided their moral decisions. Art imitates life, moreover, and what was true in these novels continues to be true for most women today. Men, in contrast, continue to be preoccupied with rules and boundaries as opposed to feelings, and they persist in believing that moral decisions made in an emotional vacuum are somehow superior to those that are not.

This theme of the emotionally free woman versus the emotionally restrained man also appears in many novels of this century. Nicole Diver in F. Scott Fitzgerald's *Tender Is the Night* (1934) and Sarah in John Fowles' *The French Lieutenant's Woman* (1969) are two more recent examples of passionate women whose decisions were guided by their hearts as much as by their heads. Emotionally these women speak not only for themselves, but for the men in their lives. Significantly, they are often punished for this.

I believe that the splitting off of the emotional life from the social archetype of masculinity (and its identification with femininity) that emerged nearly two centuries ago lies at the root of the problem for many, if not most, of the couples who have seen me professionally over the last fifteen years. In fact, I believe that as emotions became more or less the exclusive domain of women, men learned to do two things: to rely on women to express feelings for them (sometimes manipulating women so as to express feelings they themselves were incapable of expressing), and to mute their own emotionality (including their sensuality) in the interest of maintaining their self-esteem. As gender divergence became entrenched, in other words, men had little choice but to lead vicarious emotional lives. This appears to be as true today as it was when Flaubert created Emma Bovary.

Most of the men who come to my office are very conflicted about their own emotionality, and about that of women as well. They come across as decidedly ambivalent about women's capacity for emotion. Sometimes they almost worship it, especially if a woman is effectively expressing feelings for them. Many men have told me that they were attracted to their partners precisely because of the latter's capacity to express feelings such as love, joy, and excitement. So long as it is these emotions that are being expressed, and so long as the man feels that he can control them, both partners tend to be happy.

By control I mean just that, for in order to lead a vicarious emotional life, one must be able to influence the other person to express your feelings. I have worked with many men, for example, who could express either happiness or sexual passion only through their partners. One man spent thousands of dollars calling 900 numbers just so that he could listen to anonymous women "talk dirty" and pretend, for his pleasure, to get sexually aroused and have orgasms. I asked him why he did this. He replied, "Because, to tell you the truth, I get off on women's pleasure. I love to hear them groan—the louder the better. Me, I'm more or less quiet when I have sex." Another man came to the realization that the only way he was able to express joy was through his wife. He would go to great lengths to please and surprise her, and then he would share in the excitement. Left to his own devices, he explained, he was a serious fellow who had long been regarded by colleagues as lacking any passion or humor at all.

I have also known men to use women to express feelings that they have deeply repressed, including pain and grief. This is a hidden dynamic in many abusive relationships. These men can be quite cruel— and almost always emotionally cold—while acting in ways that elicit fear, pain, or sadness in their partners, who rarely suspect that they are serving as emotional proxies.

A man will tend to feel anxious when a woman begins to express feelings like anger or sadness, or when he feels that he cannot *control* her emotions. Confronted with an angry woman, an intensely sad woman, and sometimes even a sexually passionate woman, most men feel more or less intimidated. The more insecure they are, the more intimidated they will be. They will seek to avoid the intimacy inherent in such encounters; if pressed, they may get angry. This is a defensive response, reflecting their own discomfort, that is designed to scare the woman off. It often works.

It is possible to argue that the Victorians' notions about relationships were not based in the reality of their lives but instead represented a reaction to the alienation that had crept into relationships as a result of a century or more of gender divergence. Middle-class men and women in 1900 had arguably less in common, and more dissimilar orientations to life, then their counterparts in 1800. Men's positional orientation toward self and others had led them to become tuned into differences and preoccupied with their relative position. Power and control had become the dominant interpersonal themes for them. Boundaries and rules were the parameters of their lives, and emotional self-control had become the cornerstone of masculinity. They were schooled and reinforced in this from infancy onward. There were virtually no alternative models of masculinity, and the structure and rules of their peer group, starting in child-hood, operated along these lines.

Women, in contrast, had been socialized to orient themselves to others and to value and measure themselves using a relational schema. Theirs was a world of emotion and communication, where the self was defined in terms of significant relationships and where self-esteem hinged on the quality of those relationships. To be sure, however, women (especially in the middle class) needed to be cogni-zant of position in a society that had become increasingly stratified, where getting ahead had become the dominant social ethic, and where acquisitions and credentials were viewed as measures of per-sonal worth.

But despite living in a common social context, American society by 1900 had established such a long tradition of gender divergence that married life in some ways must have been something akin to an adventure in cross-cultural anthropology. Hence the emergence of "marriage manuals" and "marriage doctors"—people whose liveli-hood was based on helping men and women bridge the cultural gap that separated them. Popular books like *Married Love,* which sold in the millions, were largely efforts to help couples cross the bound-aries that gender divergence had created. By Victorian times men needed to read books in order to understand women, and vice versa. Of course it was always women, with whom communication was mainly associated, who did most of the reading about relationships, as is true today. It must no doubt have been hard for the Victorians to imagine that things were not always so, or that the explanation for their frustrations could lie anywhere but with Mother Nature.

Books about love and marriage, which are as popular today as ever, are probably most revealing of this alienation and the prob-lems of communication and the longing for intimacy that it created. If anything, Victorian romanticism may represent a poignant ex-pression of the loneliness that men and women began to feel once gender was dichotomized so severely, and once men and women went their separate ways. These issues remain alive today.

Perhaps because of his youth and the environment he lived in, young Michael, the incarcerated youth described in the first chapter, may embody the masculine ideal of toughness and emotional self-control in the most exaggerated way. He was admired by his peers for being the toughest dude in a world of tough dudes. Aside from anger that could flare forth like a deadly geyser in response to surprisingly little provocation, however, he showed little emotion. Talking to him was often like talking to a brick wall; it was positively unnerving at times. And, of course, he was stoned on marijuana almost all the time.

Paul, though inhabiting a very different world from Michael and very different on the surface in terms of personality, was also remarkably unemotional. Like Michael he had earned the admiration of his peers for being cool and tough under pressure. Instead of using fists or guns, however, his weapons were legal briefs and arguments. He had been successful in both a highly competitive law school and a highly competitive law firm, achieving this in part by drinking away his anxieties. Talking to Paul was a less anxious but no less frustrating experience than conversing with Michael. Asked how he felt in one difficult situation or another, his typical response was to fall silent, ponder, and then shrug.

Tom also prided himself on being calm, cool, and collected. A successful salesman in a competitive high–tech industry, he told me that as far back as he could remember he had possessed the ability to influence others—to "sell them," in his words, whether regarding a product or an idea. Just beneath the surface of his calm exterior I sensed a man who was very tense. When I pointed this out, however, Tom seemed genuinely surprised. He had literally never thought of himself that way.

One of the consequences of emotional restraint is alcohol and drug abuse. Men by the millions have turned to alcohol and drugs in order to quiet their discomfort, anxiety, or sadness; in order to sustain the masculine image they feel obliged to live up to; and in order to brace themselves to satisfy the competitive expectations they feel compelled to meet. The fact that men try to suppress their emotional side (and therefore seek to experience emotion vicariously through women) is one of the psychological roots of addiction. Their own emotional suppression tempts men to try to control women's emotional lives. In the process they become women's oppressors. Many men get angry when the woman in their life does not react emotionally the way they want her to. Even more ominous is some men's tendency to express, through inflicting it on others, the pain they are unable to share and of which they may even be unaware.

Addicts invariably discover that one of the first things sobriety brings is emotions that had been suppressed in part through the use of alcohol and/or drugs. Not a few have been driven back into addiction as a result of this experience. Yet recovery demands that men reclaim their emotional lives: that they allow themselves to feel, and that they give themselves the respect of having those feelings. In this way all men stand to gain from the experience of men who have recovered from addiction and who have learned to embrace their emotional selves.

4

Insecurity, Isolation, and Addiction

In the "Road Warrior" series of films the hero, Mad Max, is an archetypal survivor. Max is a man cast adrift in a desolate post-nuclear world, a place and time after civilization has literally gone up in smoke. Wandering through this world of chaos and contradiction, where remnants of sophisticated technologies lie strewn across the landscape and a fragmented society has regressed to the most primitive, merciless, and brutal level, Max makes his way alone. Ever on guard, his life is violent. If there is a theme to Max's life at all, that theme is simply survival in the ruins.

Max is one modern model of masculinity. His appeal tells us something about what many men feel, on some level, about being male today. Mad Max is, on the one hand, a good example of human adaptability. He is beyond tough. He is the ultimate competitor, because he is competing for survival. On the other hand, Max is also a man without relationships. He poses as self-sufficient but he is haunted by an intense aura of isolation and loneliness. His character is dominated by those qualities—skepticism, distrust, and a capacity to act swiftly, unilaterally, and aggressively—that enable him to make in it a hostile world, but he lacks sensitivity and connectedness.

Many of the men I talk to relate to Max. Whether they are professionals, executives, managers, or skilled workmen, they feel the pressure these days to be competitive on not only a corporate but a personal level. The workplace, they believe, is not a place where collaboration and mutual support rule. It is increasingly a place where the ethic is one for one, and none for all. Some have attempted to resolve their anxieties about this by devoting themselves to work. It is, in fact, trendy to be driven today. Making career one's first priority serves the interest of a positional orientation to life; however, it has its price.

Another film character—the husband in the popular movie *Parenthood*—expresses modern man's conflict in another way. A crisis in his life is precipitated when he gets bumped off by a competitor: when he loses an expected promotion to a younger man. His problems at work, combined with his wife's desire to have another child, bring him face-to-face with the relative roles that position and relationships play in his identity and self-esteem. This character, unlike Max, embodies what is emerging as an alternative model of masculinity. He ultimately resolves his conflict by forging a compromise between the positional and relational in his life. He fathers another child, builds intimacies with his father and son, and salvages his position through a process of renewed motivation.

As interesting as this "new man" is, many men find him difficult to identify with. It is too facile, they argue, to say that one can have it both ways (that is, have great relationships and also be an effective competitor). As an ideal, this new man who balances the positional with the relational with apparent ease may in fact be as unrealistic as the Victorian notion of love as the complete union of souls. Like the Victorian ideal, though, it says something about the hunger we feel, and about what is missing in men's lives.

If there is a single word that captures our cultural spirit at this end of the millennium, that word is *competition*. In the world of business the equivalent of Mad Max is the entrepreneur, who has been hailed as a contemporary hero archetype.[48] This corporate warrior values competitiveness above all else. He is concerned not only with maintaining his position, but with moving ever upward on the scales of success, status, and acquisition. Modern marketing techniques targeting men peddle everything from cars to cologne by appealing to the entrepreneurial image.

As a result of the modern emphasis on competition and the dominance of the positional orientation in men's lives, men have had an increasingly hard time identifying with each other on even the most basic emotional levels. The traditional vehicles for male identification and bonding—ritual and tradition, communication and storytelling, collaborative work and shared ordeal—are becoming increasingly rare. Sometimes they are artificial, as in the case of the men's "mythopoetic" movement,[49] which seeks to mimic American Indian and ancient Celtic rituals, among others, in an effort to help men bond together and experience rites of passage. It is only under unusual (and sometimes contrived) circumstances that men interact in ways that truly enable them to get into each other's shoes, to drop their positional orientation toward each other for even a little while, and to connect on an emotional level. More typically, identification between men today is shallow, based on positional factors such as common interests or shared status, and relatively fleeting. Few men tell me they actually spend significant amounts of time with male friends doing things other than team or play activities. Of course, men often say that they feel close to one another after playing a game together, going hunting together, or even attending a sporting event together; but I suggest that this is a weak connection at best. Male intimacy has been called superficial, and rightly so from this perspective. As a consequence of compulsive competitiveness, men have largely lost the ability to bond emotionally with one another.

Compulsive competition leads invariably to two problems. The first is chronic insecurity. The man whose identity and self-esteem are founded on his relative position is forever defending his place on the totem pole. The more insecure he is, the more obsessed and defensive he will be. His anxiety can get so out of hand that he becomes possessive of everything in his domain, and regards every man (and often women as well) as a threat.

A second problem that comes from compulsive competition is difficulty in the area of identification and intimacy. Competition drives men apart and makes them ever conscious of where they stand. The loneliness this produces, along with the anxiety that goes along with insecurity, are two major contributing factors in addiction.

The twentieth century increasingly has added the need to be an effective competitor onto the nineteenth-century model of men as self-controlled and resilient. In fact, I believe we have carried the concept of competition beyond the level of an ethos, making it into a veritable cult. Men have had to learn to set themselves apart from one another and to become more effective at getting more of whatever they value as symbols of self-worth: status, possessions, credentials, and so on. They have needed, more and more, to see themselves and to be seen as *different* and as *better than*. Relative position and its trappings have become the basis for men's self-worth and their sense of who they are. The price of this competitive attitude has been increasing detachment, isolation, and insecurity. Men do not want to be the same as other men any more; they want to be different, even if that means taking a lesson from the world of marketing and either exaggerating minor differences or creating artificial ones (based on what kind of car you drive, what your title is, and so forth). Similarly, men have a harder time working collaboratively now. Obviously this has profound implications for relationships, as well as for men's individual welfare. Self-esteem that is so intensely rooted in position, so ingrained in the competitive ethic, is tenuous indeed. It requires eternal vigilance and allows for precious little serenity. It isolates rather than connects us.

Ironically, many men today see their insecurity and isolation as adaptive. Survival in a competitive world, they say, demands being willing *not* to get too close to others. It requires a capacity for aggressiveness and a willingness to stand alone. Should we be surprised, then, that men have relatively little trouble expressing the one emotion—anger—that appears to facilitate competition? Anger is the emotional currency of competition, just as difference and detachment are its result.

All of the men described in the first chapter imagined that they were different and special. They were also competitive. You could say that Bill Wilson's predisposition to alcoholism was influenced by his deep sense of isolation, but that his final descent into alcoholism was triggered by his failure as a Wall Street broker. The blow to his self-esteem that the stock market crash inflicted is a common story among men. We should expect nothing else, after all, when self-esteem is founded so much on position. Bill accepted his therapist's diagnosis of his tendencies toward grandiosity— that part of himself that his therapist referred to as "His Majesty the baby."[50] And his autobiographical sketch in *Alcoholics Anonymous*[51] appears to confirm that Wilson was indeed an intensely competitive, positionally conscious man.

Interestingly enough, what saved Bill Wilson's life was a fellowship built not on the ethics of competition and detachment but on cooperation and identification. Alcoholics Anonymous is a fellowship that honors humility and surrender to a group conscience[52] rather than competitiveness and hubris. AA was from its inception a reaction against radical individualism.[53] It continues to be a militantly decentralized organization that purposefully places the welfare of the group above the individual's need for power or status. It continues to discourage focusing on differences while encouraging members to identify with one another. Seen in the historical context of gender divergence and the emergence of the social archetype of man the competitor, the birth of AA in 1935 pointed to a new way for men to see themselves and relate to each other. Born of despair, it was an idea whose time had come.

Like Bill Wilson, Paul had struggled all his life with inner dissatisfaction with his place in the world—a sure sign of insecurity. He said, "I can sum up my philosophy of life this way. I've always wanted only two things: more, and different." Paul resisted being the same as other men as intensely as any man I have ever worked with. Professionally, his fantasies did not stop at wanting to be respected and successful. He wanted to be downright famous, and he bemoaned the fact that his elected specialty of corporate law did not allow many avenues for that. It was not enough for him, similarly, to have a good relationship; he desired a love affair to rival that of Romeo and Juliet, and he felt depressed that his marriage had not lived up to that expectation. So long as he harbored such ideas, I thought, he would remain vulnerable to addiction.

For Michael, the need to be different translated very simply (but no less intensely) into wanting to make more money, to have prettier girlfriends, to drive more expensive cars, and to wear heavier gold jewelry than anyone else. How he made the money that was the key to having all these symbols of position was of little consequence to him. The one thing that could drive Michael into a rage was being told that he was "just another delinquent—nothing special."

The cult of competition and the need to be different have claimed many casualties among men. One famous example of this was the writer F. Scott Fitzgerald. A smashing success with his first novel at the age of twenty-three, Fitzgerald nevertheless died of the ravages of alcoholism at forty-four. His autobiographical comments in his essay *The Crack-Up* reveal him to be insecure at heart.

According to Fitzgerald, a turning point in his life occurred shortly after he entered Princeton. An unquestionably good student at a demanding college, Fitzgerald nevertheless chose to extend himself even further by selecting as his peer group the prestigious Triangle Club. He managed to get elected its president, but then had to give it up when he became ill and was forced to drop out of school for a year. In *The Crack-Up* he wrote about this experience and how it affected him:

> Years later I realized that my failure as a big shot in college was all right—instead of serving on committees, I took a beating on English poetry; when I got the idea of what it was about, I set about learning how to write. On Shaw's principle that "If you don't get what you like, you better like what you get," it was a lucky break—at the moment it was a harsh and bitter business to know that my career as a leader of men was over.
>
> Since that day I have not been able to fire a bad servant, and I am astonished and impressed by people who can. Some old desire for personal dominance was broken and gone. Life around me was a solemn dream, and I lived on letters I wrote to a girl in another city.[54]

For Fitzgerald, it seemed, literary success never fully compensated for his perceived failure as "a leader of men." His illness precipitated a crisis in his identity and self-esteem, which was not only positional in nature but, like many a successful man's, was in fact dependent on being a "big shot." Despite his critical and financial successes he remained, as his sad commentary suggests, as discontent and anxious as any other insecure man.

Thanks to the way we socialize boys, competition makes itself felt early in their lives. I can remember very clearly the tension that ran as an undercurrent in the excitement of sports throughout my own childhood and adolescence. Few men will not relate to the (often unexpressed) fear of being labeled a loser at sports, or of being chosen last to join a team. Boys and men's games are dominated by a concern for rules and boundaries.[55] These not only set the stage for controlled competition but are actually a metaphor for male relationships and men's positional orientation toward life. Play, for boys, has an edge to it that does not seem to be as prevalent in that of girls. This same dynamic remains dominant throughout men's lives.

As the passage from Fitzgerald's essay reveals, a man's identity boils down to a niche or position within a competitive social hierarchy. His self-esteem is contingent upon being able to maintain this position. It is characterized by a sense of territoriality and is marked off by boundaries of class, status, credentials, and so on. Men express this territorial and positional nature of their self-esteem in their words and actions; it raises its head all the time in the therapist's office. One woman talked to me about her frustrations in getting her husband, Kevin, to communicate with her whenever there was anything remotely like a crisis in the family. At these times, she complained, Kevin never wanted to talk about it. His pattern was to avoid communicating by saying he was either too tired or too busy. If pressed, he would get irritable. As a last resort he would throw up his hands and say, "You decide!" in a way that implied he did not really care one way or the other.

The conflict that this couple was having was directly related to differences between men and women in terms of how their identities are formed and the foundations of their self-esteem. Kevin's wife was seeking mutuality in her marriage, which involves making decisions by consensus. This in turn requires a great deal of communication. As Deborah Tannen has pointed out, when decisions are made by consensus and through communication, women feel intimate and cared for.[56]

But for the past century and a half, male identity and self-esteem have been based more on power and control than on mutuality. Men tend to associate mutuality, in fact, with weakness and loss of control. The hidden dynamic in this and countless other marriages has to do with the man's acute sensitivity to who is "in charge" or "on top." Kevin preferred either to make decisions himself or to hand over the power to his wife to decide. This latter approach was in effect a way for him to maintain apparent control while sparing his self-esteem. The third alternative, decision by consensus, was the most uncomfortable for Kevin psychologically, as it is for the majority of men who show up for marriage counseling.

The way that Kevin described his work was also typical and revealing of the way men approach identity and self-esteem. "I have a certain amount of expertise in my specific area," he explained. "It's a very specialized area, and over the years I've more or less been able to carve out my own space within the agency. People pretty much leave me alone now."

The work of "carving out" an identity begins in childhood, but it takes a decidedly more serious turn during adolescence. Competence and competitiveness become as crucial to adolescent boys as relationships and mutuality are to adolescent girls. Whereas teenage girls seek to establish a network of relationships that becomes a prototype for communicative intimacy (and the cornerstone of their identity), boys strive to define themselves in terms of a set of assets and competencies that largely set them apart from one another and define their relative position in the social hierarchy. To some extent girls today are becoming caught up in this male dynamic as well, and many are experiencing the stresses that result from trying to serve two masters (relating and competing). This, of course, is the same bind that men are struggling with as they seek to redefine masculinity.

Before I go further, it would perhaps be useful to define a little more specifically what I mean when I refer to insecure men. By this I mean men whose sense of identity and self-esteem are tenuous; they are more or less always worried about their position relative to other men. Insecure men are much more tuned in to contrasting themselves with others and identifying differences than to comparing and finding similarities. In other words, they become better at detaching and separating than at identifying and bonding. And because men's identities are based on relative position anyway, the insecure man's relationships are marked by constant tension, distancing, anxiety, and loneliness. Since the appreciation of similarities and identification are the bases of intimacy, it is easy to see why the insecure man typically does not feel close or connected to others.

Let us look more specifically, though, at the signs and symptoms of insecurity in men. What follows is a capsule description of an insecure man's personality. Keep in mind that insecurity is more of a dimension than a category, and that men vary a great deal in the extent of their insecurity. My point here is that the positional orientation lends itself to insecurity, but that there are many differences in degree.

I should also make the point that from my perspective, insecurity and what might be called low self-esteem are pretty much synonymous. I prefer the former term, however, since I believe it describes more vividly the dominant feeling that men have when their positional orientation to self and others is tenuous. It is not only that their self-esteem (their feelings about their own worth) is low, but that it is shaky. The word *insecure* captures this nicely.

The Insecure Man

Grandiose. Grandiosity is perhaps the most common personal characteristic of the insecure man. To compensate for anxiety about his relative position, the insecure man exaggerates his relative worth, ability, and so on. Because he is also isolated, the insecure man not only stops maturing but may actually become more infantile (regressed) over time. Qualities associated with grandiosity and infantilism include an inflated sense of self-importance, low tolerance for frustration, and the need for immediate gratification. This is the "His Majesty the baby" profile to which Bill Wilson's analyst referred.

Critical. Being critical goes hand in hand with being grandiose. Both qualities serve the same purpose, which is to create a false sense of superiority. Tom, the salesman whose relationship problems were described in the first chapter, was described by his girlfriend as very critical. "He always seems to think he can do things better than me," she said one time, "but he forgets that he's screwed up royally at times." She went on to accuse Tom of being critical of her friends, an attitude she felt they sensed that distanced them from him, and indirectly from her as well.

Possessive. The insecure man is territorial and possessive. He is jealous, often ungenerous with affection and support, and unsympathetic. His heart is filled with envy of what others have, and not infrequently he indulges in self-pity over what he does not have. His resentment can come out as meanness or vindictiveness. In relationships he is preoccupied with his "space," his possessions, or his "freedom" (which he guards like a possession).

Defensive. The insecure man is think-skinned and easily hurt. He is usually vigilant for words or actions that might threaten to pierce his fragile self-esteem. If he perceives that he is being criticized, he may counterattack viciously, or he may give the offender the cold shoulder and withdraw. The sensitivity of the insecure man often betrays the self-confidence that his grandiosity would suggest. Many insecure but successful men surprise and dismay their partners with the degree to which they react to the slightest confrontation or criticism.

Distrustful. As being critical goes with being grandiose, so does distrust go with being defensive. For the insecure man, trusting others amounts to foolishness. He spends a great deal of time looking for reasons to justify his distrust, and he usually finds them. What he often fails to see, however, is that he holds others up to a standard of trustworthiness that he himself probably could not satisfy. In effect, he expects people to be more than human, and then holds it against them when they are not.

Rigid. The insecure man regards compromise as a loss. In his world there are only two ways of doing things: his way, and the wrong way. He is described variously as stubborn, bullheaded, and dominating. Obsessed with winning, with being in control, and with being right, he can be either cleverly manipulating or brutishly intimidating in order to get his way.

Obsessively Self-Reliant. The insecure man resists mutuality and consensus. He acts as if it is really possible to be an island unto oneself. He acts as though human beings are not fundamentally social creatures, dependent on one another for everything from making babies to escaping loneliness. He makes self-reliance into more than a virtue—for him, it is an obsession. Decision making is power; he prefers to make decisions without talking about them first, and he resents being asked to do so. What his partner seeks as mutuality he interprets as threat to his self-reliance and therefore resists.

Compulsive. Compulsiveness is the last refuge of the desperate man—the man who seeks to control the uncontrollable. Life confronts men with limitations every day. The man whose self-esteem is more secure is more likely to accept these limitations. The insecure man also experiences his lack of control over many things, but instead of accepting this as a part of life, he compensates by becoming compulsive. Virtually every addict I have ever met was compulsive in some way or another. Often, they were still compulsive in recovery. The underlying dynamic of compulsiveness is essentially the same as that of addiction, in that both offer temporary comfort and escape. If we cannot control the world, then we can either make it go away chemically or try to control something else, like our relationships, our children, or our home.

Isolated. Precisely because they are so preoccupied with being in control, self-reliant, and superior, insecure men invariably suffer intense, often secret feelings of isolation and loneliness. Deep down they do not feel as though they belong. Forever on the outside looking in, they are, ironically, prisoners within a castle of their own making. They not only find it difficult to identify with other men but actually are highly ambivalent about doing so, for to be able to identify truly and deeply means dropping any pretext of superiority or difference. Insecure men have great difficulty opening themselves to intimacy for similar reasons. Though on the surface some insecure men present a veneer of openness and mutuality, the true test of security comes when it is time to make important decisions through communication, compromise, and consensus. The more a man is able to do this, I suggest, the more free he will be in the long run from the constraints of a rigidly positional orientation toward self and others.

The above synopsis of the insecure man may describe you or any number of other men you know. If so, I hope that your first reaction is not to pathologize either them or yourself. Insecurity, I would emphasize again, is endemic to the male role and our concept of masculinity as it has evolved. It is the rule, not the exception, among men. That is not to say that it is not a problem; on the contrary, from my perspective it *is* the problem with men. Since it is so ubiquitous, however, it is not something to feel unusual about.

In assessing your own insecurity (I am not so sure how well we can assess that of others), try to be as honest with yourself as possible. Start by doing a thorough inventory of yourself in terms of the qualities listed above. Try to identify specific examples of behaviors and situations that illustrate any of these qualities in you. Which situations tend to bring them out the most? Obviously, the more the description fits you, the more work you will need to do in order to increase your self-esteem and your sense of security.

Next, think of times when you are most open about your inner feelings, and times when you are most open to talking and making important decisions through consensus and compromise. This is what intimacy and mutuality are all about. It is the direction you need to go in if you want to escape the pain of insecurity.

Insecurity is associated with chronic anxiety and discontent, with loneliness and isolation, and often with boredom as well. As a man moves away from insecurity, his life becomes dominated more by the emotional themes of serenity, intimacy, and passion for work. I will look much more closely at these things in later chapters.

The origins of insecurity are not overly mysterious. Given the predisposition to it that is created by the way we socialize boys into men, it is little wonder that it is so common. At the same time, though, it is a tendency that can be made much worse by abuse, neglect, and abandonment. Most recovering men have long tales to tell in this regard. While it is important that they not slip into ruinous self-pity, it is also vital that their stories be validated, just as we need to validate the stories of pain and grief that most men have to tell as a consequence of being raised to be a man.

5

The New Male

Tim and Mary had been married for fourteen years and had three children, who ranged in age from six to twelve. Tim was a very successful and very hardworking executive. Mary had a small business of her own that, although less lucrative by far than her husband's, nevertheless earned her a respectable income and a great deal of personal satisfaction. Tim worked long hours and, according to Mary, complained about it all the time, though he kept at it and kept on getting ahead.

As successful as he was, Mary explained, Tim had always struck her as being very insecure about his work. "As long as I've known him," she said, "Tim has always worried about losing his job. No matter how big his bonuses are, no matter how good his evaluations are, or what kind of promotion he's gotten, he's always telling me that he doesn't know how long it will last. He works harder than any man I know. It seems that the job runs his life, instead of vice versa. Do you know what I mean? He says he likes his work, but I can't see where he gets any joy from it. He seems to live in constant dread of getting bumped off tomorrow. Are all men that way?"

In fact, Tim was insecure and addicted to work. It was not only the long hours he put in that were symptomatic of this, but his other behavior. For example, work always came first in his life. He was preoccupied with it—married to his job the same way that some men are married to the bottle. This is the essence of addiction: it is something that we become preoccupied with, that dominates our thoughts and actions to the exclusion of other things that would benefit us. Addiction destroys the balance in our lives and controls us even when we would rather be doing or thinking about something else, and even when it costs us in terms of our health and welfare.

Tim liked to say that he worked as hard as he did for his family, but that was a cover-up for his addiction. Men use this excuse a lot, but when work makes their marriage and family life suffer, it is important to look at that kind of statement critically. In reality Tim had insisted for years that his wife and children take a back seat to his preoccupation with work. For fourteen years his family had never been able to count on him being home at a predictable time. His typical workday started at five-thirty in the morning. He would be in the office by seven, a good hour or more ahead of everyone else. (Was he doing *that* for his family?) He would get home anywhere between six and seven-thirty in the evening.

Whenever he tried to change in response to Mary's complaints about working too hard, Tim acted like what alcoholics in recovery have come to call a "dry drunk,"[57] a syndrome that describes the personality of any addict who tries to stop without working on the spiritual and psychological issues that drive the obsession or compulsion. While trying to relax or to focus on some family activity, Tim was forever thinking about work, and he was irritable and distracted most of the time. He would even sneak in some work when Mary and the kids went out, and would encourage them to do so just so he could work. On vacations he would bring along his attaché case ("Just in case I have some time on my hands," he would say).

If anyone or anything interfered with Tim's work—like a child getting sick or having an accident—he'd get testy. Mary expressed her resentment at this. "You'd think I was calling him at his girlfriend's house!" she exclaimed, "Or that I'm interrupting him at work to ask him if I should make rice or baked potatoes with dinner!"

At home Tim was critical of the children (and of Mary) whenever they did not behave the way he thought they should. He was a scolding and aloof father, prone to losing his temper. He blew up at the children regularly, usually for being messy. As a result, Mary said, the kids disappeared quickly after their father got home. As she saw it, they had more or less learned to ignore him. If she tried to explain this to him, however, Tim would blow up at her.

Tim came across as feeling sorry for himself a lot. His favorite expressions always seemed to begin with "If it weren't for me . . . " and ended in predicting some disaster that would befall the family if he didn't work so hard. I could understand why his kids had learned to ignore him, and I could sense the alienation that had crept into his marriage to Mary.

He also came across as self-absorbed and grandiose. Tim's insecurity, I later learned, came in part from being raised by a father who was very much the same way. It was compounded by some early frustrations in college, which had struck a major blow to his self-esteem. He had started off as a science major but switched into business when he did poorly in his first two calculus courses. Tim experienced this as a devastating personal failure: it largely destroyed his positional image of himself as someone who was more intelligent than other men, and it raised inner doubts about his ability as a competitor that had nagged him ever since.

Tim suffered from periodic bouts of insomnia and occasional anxiety attacks that he still sometimes mistook for heart attacks. More than once Mary had rushed him to the emergency room in the middle of the night, only to be told after a series of tests that his heart was fine, although his anxiety level was not. These were some of the negative consequences, I explained, of both his insecurity and his work addiction.

Tim and Mary came to see me after he discovered, about a year after it ended, that she had engaged in a brief affair. He was angry but also devastated, and though I quickly surmised why Mary had done it, I could not help feeling a little sorry for Tim. It was like college and his father all over again—an experience that told him he just was not good enough. Although he had carved out an identity and built a life-style that was the envy of many of his friends, inwardly Tim had the typical hungry heart that drives men to be just as he was. He was full of anger at Mary, but privately he admitted to me that he had always feared that his obsession with work would lead precisely to this. In their heart of hearts, most addicts know exactly what they are. "I know I'm a bear," he said. "I know I think too much about work. I know I'm insecure as hell. I know that Mary's right—my kids do blow me off. I know all these things, but I can't seem to change. Honestly, I don't know how many times I've sworn to myself that tomorrow it will be different, only to do the exact same thing the minute I walk in the door. To tell you the truth, I'd more or less given up on changing. But I know I have to. Maybe you can help me. I don't want to lose Mary."

What Tim was asking for was nothing less than my help in becoming a new man. His dilemma was familiar. As a modern man, he was heir to a nearly two-century-long tradition of gender divergence that has shaped society's ideas about the nature of masculinity and femininity. On the one hand, we have come to think of a man as someone who is strong and resilient, who is emotionally restrained, who is competitive, and who is perhaps most of all in control. On the other hand, men are experiencing growing pressure to change, to become more androgynous, and to be able to be nurturing, sensitive, communicative, and compromising.

By and large, modern man's relationships, especially with his fellow men, are competitive. His identity and consequently his self-esteem are dependent on maintaining his niche in the world. He is more or less forever conscious of his place on the totem pole and his need to defend it. Inwardly he feels anxious and isolated, of course, but outwardly he carefully maintains his image of strength and confidence. At the same time he is being asked more and more to open himself to mutuality and intimacy, both of which make him decidedly nervous.

Tim's story is not unusual. There are innumerable men out there today who are struggling to redefine their sense of who they are and to make themselves more secure. It is anything but unusual for them to feel pressure to do this from those who are closest to them and who are unhappy with the quality of the relationship.

Though the themes that dominate their struggles are clear, the direction in which men need to move has not been so clear. In a truly ironic twist, many men have decided that their problem is that they have become too passive and that what they need to become is tougher and more competitive. Books about men and the male dilemma have become dominated by images of warriors and kings. At times their titles reveal the male conflict poignantly, though, as when they employ images such that of a gentle warrior or a knight without armor. The result for the individual man is often more confusion than direction.

In truth, the driving force behind the current men's movement probably was the women's liberation movement that is associated with the tumultuous 1960s but had its real beginnings in the post–World War I era. From my perspective as a therapist over the past fifteen years, it has been women more than men that have been the motivating force behind changes in relationships, with men moving along the path reluctantly at best. Women have been driven to change as a consequence of the breakdown of the Victorian female sex role. Having entered the competitive and positional world of men in vast numbers, they have probably been changed by that world and orientation more than they have changed either one. No doubt men's rigid adherence to the positional orientation has contributed to this; if men were to change, women would have more options than simply to become like men in order to succeed in the world of business and industry.

In response to the changing role and identity of women, men have reacted with confusion, fear, and anger. Recently, some men have begun to react in a more creative and truly empowering way that involves exploring ways of redefining themselves. This is the direction, I think, we need to go in.

Briefly, what men need to do is to broaden and balance the base on which they establish their identity and build self-esteem. Healthy self-esteem can indeed be based, in part, on an awareness of our real talents and abilities. A positional orientation has long been the mainstay of male identity and self-esteem. There is nothing wrong with it per se, and I am hardly suggesting that men abandon it. Similarly, neither is there anything inherently wrong in competition, or in striving to do well. The current cult of competition, however, pushes men toward an extreme positional orientation. It makes relative position a decidedly insecure basis for self-esteem. It also limits men's capacity to open themselves to intimacy.

Even many so-called liberated men feel anxious when a woman's abilities encroach upon the territory that defines their identity and self-esteem. And many men have fallen into substance abuse and addiction when circumstances have threatened their sense of position. These pitfalls of the male role reflect the insecurity that it engenders. Of course, a personal history of abuse, abandonment, or neglect only serves to drive men more desperately toward a positional stance.

In order to be more secure, men need to explore relational bases for self-esteem and identity. This does not mean abandoning a positional orientation altogether, but it does mean being willing to let go of it at times in the interest of exploring and developing relational pathways to self-esteem. It also means letting go of a positional orientation in order to experience intimacy. When a man is able to do this, he accomplishes several things psychologically. First, he reduces the chronic insecurity that comes from constantly having to be vigilant and to defend one's position against a never-ending lineup of competitors. Second, it reduces the sense of isolation that haunts so many men, inviting them to bury their sorrow in one obsession or another. Last of all, it opens the door to men becoming truly androgynous, to their being able to establish relationships based on mutuality and to deepen their sense of connectedness to other men.

What will the new male look like? To be sure, he will still capture some of the spirit of being male that predates even the gender divergence that has so affected men since the nineteenth century. For me, however, that spirit includes many qualities that are not necessarily the exclusive domain of men. One of these has to do with adventure and challenge. The need for mutuality and intimacy, and even for intimacy, does not have to mean that men will forgo their desire to wander and explore, or to rise to challenges. Nor will it eliminate in any way the need for male bonding. On the contrary, it may deepen the bonds between men as they are able to define themselves relationally as well as positionally.

Writers such as Jack Kerouac,[58] Robert Pirsig,[59] Peter Matthiessen,[60] and William Least Heat Moon[61] have all written accounts capturing the spirit of freedom and adventure that can be a vital part of the male psyche. Such other qualities as perseverance, moral determination, and courage, which of late have been overshadowed by the need to compete and to win regardless of character, will also be part of the new male. At the same time the increasingly androgynous male will be one whose personality and character strike a greater balance between competition and collaboration, between personal effectiveness and mutuality.

To be sure, this will not be accomplished without sacrifice. We should not be so naive as to believe that men, any more than women, can be all things at once. What will have to be let go is the obsession with competitiveness and place, along with radical individualism and the illusion of self-sufficiency. Again I would suggest that the emergence of Alcoholics Anonymous as a fellowship of peers—and whose traditions and structure challenge the positional approach to problems of living that demand a differential relationship between a doctor and a patient—was a harbinger of the direction that men would have to go in if they hoped to live a truly sober life. This began by essentially rejecting the very foundations of Victorian masculinity, as these quotes indicate:

> The philosophy of self-sufficiency is not paying off. Plainly enough, it is a bone-crushing juggernaut whose final achievement is ruin.[62]

> The first requirement [for recovery] is that we be convinced that any life run on self-will can hardly be a success.[63]

As we approach the task of becoming "new men," therefore, we must be willing to approach it with a certain amount of humility. This simple virtue seems almost to have gotten lost in this age of competitiveness and grandiosity. Yet humility is essential to change; without it, you will no doubt resist every suggestion this book has to offer.

The second and third parts of this book present guidelines for how men can explore a relational (as opposed to positional) orientation to self and others. They are not an alternative program for recovery from addiction. If anything, they represent a series of pathways that men in recovery could pursue in order to strengthen recovery and reduce their vulnerability to addiction. I believe that a positional approach to self-esteem is a viable way—but not the only way—to define oneself and to build self-esteem. The remainder of this book is devoted to an exploration of alternative ways for men to define who they are and to establish their worth.

PART TWO

Men and Self-Esteem

All neurotics have a childhood behind them in which they were moved by doubt regarding the achievement of full masculinity. The renunciation of masculinity, however, appears to the child as synonymous with femininity, an opinion which holds not only for the child, but also for the greater part of our culture. Thus a wide area of originally childish value judgments is given. Accordingly, any form of uninhibited aggression, activity, potency, power, and the traits of being brave, free, rich, aggressive, or sadistic can be considered as masculine.

—Alfred Adler[64]

6

Fathers and Sons

In describing the psychodynamics of neurosis, the psychoanalyst Alfred Adler refers to *all* people. Yet is seems obvious that his words apply most specifically to men. In identifying neurosis as related to feelings of inadequacy, I believe Adler was on the right track. I prefer the word *insecure,* since I feel that it captures better the sense of anxiety and isolation that characterizes men whom Adler would have labeled neurotic. Insecurity reflects the problems of self-esteem that result when identity becomes rigidly dependent on a positional orientation toward oneself and others.

In this part of the book I will explore the origins of self-esteem and describe ways in which men can go about creating a better balance in their self-esteem. If they do this, they will discover that they are less anxious, less obsessed with control, less compulsive, and less insecure in general. Equally important, they will reduce their vulnerability to addiction. In the process they will also begin to open themselves to forming attachments to other men, and to experiencing intimacy in their relationships. I begin by taking a look at the beginnings of men's sense of self and their self-esteem.

I have only the barest recollection of one of my two grandfathers. He was my father's father, and he died when I was five or six. My one clear memory is of the two of us, he ahead and me behind, pacing endlessly up and down the length of his living room in what was then called a "railroad apartment" (so named because each room led directly to the next, with no external hallway, so that to get to the last room you had to pass first through all the others). I have a recollection of heavy, dark, upholstered furniture and drawn drapes with a floral design, whose translucence bathed the room in a dusky light.

I have been told that this grandfather loved me very much and enjoyed my companionship. I believe it—I can feel it still. I also learned, much later, that all the while we were pacing like that he was dying of cancer. I have a vague image in my mind of a face that could have been worried, beneath a bald head that I loved to stare at, atop a body that seemed immensely tall at the time.

He may have been dying, but he never let on to me. Whenever his eye caught mine he would smile down at me, pause for a moment, then continue his pacing. We did not talk much. I have been told that if my grandmother tried to shoo me out of the room he would tell her to let me be, and that when my parents said it was time to go he would tell them to let me stay a while longer.

I have memories of us pacing together on more than one occasion; and then he was gone. I do not really remember the funeral. But I do recall his face, and the warm feeling I got from just being there with him, pacing back and forth.

My maternal grandfather lived longer; I was about fourteen when he died. He was a tall man with a square jaw and broad shoulders, deep-set eyes, and a full head of dark hair. I remember my mother commenting when he died that he still had all his hair, and that there was hardly any gray in it. My father sarcastically said he probably dyed it with shoe polish.

This grandfather was an alcoholic, prone to binges and frequent periods of unemployment. I can recall that he was forever getting a new job—usually something menial, like a janitor. It never occurred to me to ask why he changed jobs so often. When we visited on holidays, someone would always ask him what his latest job was, or if he had one. He always answered them politely. In my upwardly mobile family he was, to say the least, a black sheep. My father absolutely could not tolerate him and did little to conceal his animosity; the anger in him was palpable at times. I learned much later that my mother and her siblings had feared their father when they were young and on more than one occasion they had literally hidden beneath their beds to escape his drunken wrath. Perhaps that was why my father disliked him so. But because my relationship with him was spared all that, I always liked my "Grandpa."

One thing I liked about Grandpa was that he thought I was just about the smartest, best-looking, most talented kid that ever was, period. Whenever I visited him (which was always too rare for me and too often for my father), I would dazzle him with my latest intellectual achievement. Drawing a simple diagram of an atom was enough to knock his socks off. He would carry it into the kitchen, corral my grandmother, and extol my genius, predicting with confidence that I would someday be a great scientist.

Aside from his thinking I was great (and telling me so), I am most indebted to Grandpa for taking the time to show me the world, such as it was in that part of Brooklyn where I spent my early years. He had no car, so wherever we went we always walked. We did this only when we were alone, meaning whenever my parents were not around to ask too many questions about where we were going or what we were doing.

With a look in his eye that made my whole body tingle with excitement, Grandpa would set his tall, lanky frame down at the kitchen table, lean back, and ask me if I wanted to go for a walk. That was our code word. To me it meant one thing: adventure. While I could barely contain myself, he would casually tell my grandmother that we were going "for a nice long walk." She never asked a question; she just nodded. Looking back, I suppose she was glad to be rid of him for a while.

It did not bother me at all to have to take two or more strides to Grandpa's one as he moved at a good clip through the streets of west Brooklyn, near the East River. It did not matter at all how far we went; in fact, as far as I was concerned, the farther the better. Along the way I knew I could count on making several brief stops. These were opportunities for Grandpa to rest up for a few minutes and chat with one or another of his cronies. To a one these were men with craggy faces, bloodshot eyes, and scruffy chins—men who were long used to earning whatever they earned by the sweat of their backs, who always had a certain sadness about them despite their coarse and exaggerated laughter, and who bore their defeat in the struggle for success with a small measure of dignity. Many, I realize now, must have known struggles with the bottle, as my grandfather did. Regardless of their problems and histories, though, they were my grandfather's friends, and I accepted them at face value. Every time he would introduce me it would be with a prideful voice and a pat on the head. Each man, no matter how many times he had met me before, would always look down at me and nod. Sometimes they would smile. There was a sense of validation that was communicated by those little gestures that is hard for me to describe.

My walks with Grandpa took me to places that no one else would have. My father was much too busy for such things, and I suspect he would have disapproved in any case. He spent what seemed to me like all of his time working, earning the money that eventually accumulated into a down payment on the Long Island "development" house that we lived in for many years. In this house I finally had my own cherished room, and the demands of work and a time-consuming commute increased my separation from my father.

Once, when I expressed an interest in a certain bridge that my father always drove across on his way to dropping me off at my grandparents' apartment, Grandpa looked down and said, "Want to walk across it?" I couldn't believe my ears. Did I want to walk across a bridge? Was he kidding?

I can still feel the vibration of the concrete walkway beneath my feet as I imagine us treading along the narrow sidewalk that ran along one side of the bridge. A sturdy wrought-iron fence separated us from the buzzing traffic on one side, and a second, heavier one separated us from the streets below. As we headed upward, the view changed from one of tenement facades to roofs and then a patchwork quilt of backyards, more brown than green, with an occasional shrub or stilted tree, and crisscrossed with a parade of laundry strung from long lines. Finally, as we neared the top, the concrete roadway gave way to a heavy metal gridwork that made the car tires whine loudly.

We stopped at the very top, and I looked down over the rail. The backyards and streets were gone. Below me lay an expanse of brown-black dirt and asphalt—the banks of the river. Through the middle of this scene the mysterious black ribbon of water curved, its current visible in places in small eddies. As I stared down at it, a small piece of wood drifted by. I heard Grandpa say something to me, but the traffic was too noisy to make out his words. Then he tapped my shoulder and I looked back and up at him, meeting his eyes. He smiled, then pointed the way back down. I sighed and followed him.

My father was what you would call a solid man. Reliable, hardworking, and ambitious, he worked his way up from meager working class beginnings to become a corporate executive. He put in long hours without complaint and tended to be stoic about the wear and tear caused by four or more hours a day of daily commuting to and from New York City. Though he was frugal and I sometimes resented it, he never denied us nearly as much as he denied himself. He took pride in his accomplishments and endured the competitiveness of corporate life seemingly without rancor.

Dad was one of the first of the breed of commuters that eventually seemed to make up the bulk of the adult male population of suburban Long Island. Up at five in the morning, ready and waiting for the car pool by six, the only hard evidence of his existence was the empty coffee cup he would leave behind in the kitchen sink each morning. By the time he got home we had already had dinner, and I would be busy with my homework. Without exaggeration, I doubt that we exchanged more than ten or fifteen words a day for years. It got so that we related through silence. Our relationship was based on shared work, or simply on being together. When we drove somewhere together, for example, we exchanged few words, and these were almost always about household business. My father liked to think out loud about what kind of fertilizer we should be spreading at that time of year, or whether we should raise the lawnmower setting now that the dry season was upon us. It was taken for granted that I would either help or, as I got older, actually do much of the work involved.

If my father had ever actually tried to start a conversation with me, I would have been shocked. I do not believe I would have known how to have a conversation with him. Still, I took every opportunity to be with him, accompanying him when he ran errands on weekends and assisting him with projects around the house. Once in a while, in the summers, he would show up halfway through one of my Little League games, his tie hanging loose around his neck and his white shirtsleeves rolled up. I remember feeling more nervous than usual whenever he was there, not because he was critical, but because of the unusualness of it. Afterward he would pack my bike into the trunk of the car, and we would drive home. He would talk a little about baseball in general, being an avid fan and a former high school jock. Sometimes he offered a tip or two about my play, and once in a while he would compliment me.

My motivation in sharing these personal experiences is not merely sentimental. The point I wish to make is that my early relationships with the most significant men in my life affected me in many ways. Sometimes we assume that for such relationships to be formative, they need to involve a great deal of contact and verbal communication. This is not so. Boys seem to "imprint" themselves onto the men in their lives, copying them and looking to them as important sources for forming an identity and building self-esteem.

My grandfathers and my father together taught me a great deal about being a man. I derived my most basic attitudes toward emotion, work, and relationships from them. I also learned what kind of *conditions* were associated with approval, and which could build my self-esteem from a positional perspective. Hard work, success, and a certain stoic toughness were values that became absorbed into my identity.

Today, many men I talk to express some degree of resentment that their relationships with their fathers were not deeper. Some men had fathers who made my own seem accessible and involved by comparison. Others suffered outright rejection, ridicule, and abuse. I do not intend to dismiss the pain or even the resentment of these men; perhaps I was one of the fortunate ones. Still, I wish to make one point concerning the importance of the father-son relationship to identity development and self-esteem in boys. Mothers can provide (or deny) love, nurturance, guidance, and knowledge, and they may represent an important model of womanhood for their sons. They cannot, however, provide the same basis for identity development that fathers can. Years of working with adolescent boys have taught me that they seek to model themselves after adult males just as I did, and they will readily adopt a role model or even create one in their imagination in order to satisfy this need. I have known youths who modeled fathers they had literally never met, having constructed an image of them simply on the basis of stories.

A second and equally important point I wish to make with these stories is that a boy's early relationships with significant men not only teach him the how-tos of manhood, but also establish the orientation toward self and others that he will use in building his own self-esteem. For me, being tough and stoic, being successful in academics and on the athletic field, and acquiring certain credentials as signs of status became significant dimensions of identity. My self-esteem in turn became tied to achieving and maintaining these things. This, then, was my *positional identity,* which led directly to specific conditions for self-esteem. When I met these conditions I could feel pride; when I failed I would feel shame.

What is most significant for men is whether, as boys, they are able to establish any degree of identity at all from a relational orientation. Severe abuse, neglect, and rejection from the men that boys attempt to become attached to can prevent this. In that case, several things happen. First, the boy is left to establish an identity and self-esteem solely in a positional way. This leads to insecurity and isolation. Second, the boy will tend to turn more or less exclusively to women, as opposed to men, for personal validation and to meet his need for attachment.

Michael, the youth described in the first chapter, was a case in point. Having been cruelly rejected by his father, he had nevertheless modeled him, becoming a drug dealer and a tough guy. Making money and basking in its power were core elements of his identity. His self-esteem was rooted in being a "high roller" (a major drug dealer), in providing money for his impoverished family, and in being desirable to women. On the other hand, Michael had not been able to form an attachment to his father—or to any other adult male, for that matter. As a consequence, his relationships with males were strictly competitive (reflecting his exclusively positional orientation). He used men only to measure his worth in comparison to them, with money and aggressiveness being his primary dimensions of comparison. In contrast, he turned to women to validate his interpersonal desirability. Naturally, since he was dependent on them for this, he became very controlling and possessive of his relationships with women, including with his own mother.

In addition to modeling personal qualities associated with manhood, my early relationships with the significant men in my life enabled me to form mutual attachments to them. Aside from being liked by my maternal grandfather for being smart, I got the clear feeling that he simply liked being in a relationship with me. Our relationship itself was important to both of us; being together was the basis of our bonding. For me the smiles in my grandfathers' eyes and the fact of my father's mere presence at my baseball games were validating. They formed the basis of my being able to form attachments with men, to integrate those attachments into my identity, and to utilize them, in however limited a way, as part of the basis for my self-esteem.

What you could call a person's *relational identity,* then, is based in the significant attachments he or she has built. The self-esteem that emanates from this identity is considerably less conditional than are positional identity and self-esteem. It is not dependent on performance, or on maintaining some position in the hierarchy. It is based instead on maintaining the relationship itself, in affirming the attachment that bonds two people together.

Men can (and do) experience relational self-esteem, as they do indeed base part of their identity on relationships. Because of the historic fact of gender divergence and the development of complementary concepts of masculinity and femininity, however, men have for a long time been pressed much more toward the positional than the relational orientation, and consequently toward positional versus relational identities and self-esteem. The result is that men are more vulnerable to insecurity and all it brings with it, including addiction.

It strikes me as significant that men talk so little about self-esteem and attachment, and that surprisingly little is written about it. It is as though self-esteem and attachment were not issues for men, when of course they are. At the same time, I am struck by the fact that we seem to talk a great deal about men's "self-confidence" or "egos." These terms impress me as coming from a positional orientation; they connote an element of competitiveness, or at least of relative strength. Without self-confidence or ego, for example, men are apt to experience difficulty in their efforts to establish and defend a positional identity.

When we attempt to speak about men's identity and self-esteem from a relational perspective, however, there is a notable lack of meaningful constructs. Men by and large do not have a language for construing relationships from a relational as opposed to a positional perspective. They speak very little about their attachments to other men, and may not even be able to make much sense of that concept. In contrast, they readily relate to such concepts as being allies, teammates, colleagues, or competitors, all of which have a positional connotation. For much the same reason, men associate intimacy more with experiences that involve alliance or shared ordeal than they do with relational concepts like emotional openness or communication.

Significantly, all of the men described in the first chapter could have articulated the conditions on which their identities and self-esteem were founded, and each of them in their own way had satisfied those conditions. Yet each of them had a hungry heart. Each of them was insecure and lonely, and every one of them was an addict. The reasons, I believe, had very much to do with the lack of balance in their identities, and in the one-sided manner in which they tried to maintain their self-esteem. The implication, for me at least, is clear: the direction that men need to pursue in order to reduce their vulnerability to addiction, and also their insecurity, is toward balancing positional identity and self-esteem with a relational counterpart.

This has not generally been the tack taken by therapists when working with insecure men. On the contrary, they often do just the opposite, trying to help men become more assertive, more warriorlike, or more independent. In effect, they try to enhance men's positional identities. This is not an entirely useless approach, but it has clear limitations.

Before moving on, the reader should take some time to reflect on this issue of early attachments and their relationship to identity and self-esteem. The following are offered as food for thought, in the hope that they will stimulate a productive inner dialogue.

- To the best of your memory, what was your earliest (childhood) relationship with your father like? Was he nurturing and warm, or cold and rejecting? Did you gravitate toward him, and how did he respond to that? Would you say you were "attached" to him?
- Were there any other adult men in your life with whom you spent time, and to whom you think you formed an attachment?
- Attachments are always mutual. One test of attachment is that you feel that you are important to the other person, just as he or she is important to you. What early relationships with men met this criterion?
- In what ways did your early relationships with your father and other men in your life set conditions for your self-esteem? By *conditions,* I mean personal qualities or standards that you learned to associate with approval and respect. We model

many of these conditions from the men in our lives, and we also absorbed them by things we hear. Thus we can learn to associate being rich, having an education, being strong, and so forth with approval and respect. Who did you model the most, and what were some of the conditions you took on as a basis for your own self-esteem?

- Our positional identity comes from knowing who we are in comparison to others, especially other men. How much of your self-esteem today is tied into this idea of comparing yourself to other men? What are the key dimensions that you think set you apart from other men, and which are the cornerstones of your self-esteem?

- Our relational identity stems from our sense of being important to others not so much for what we do or what we have, but for who we are. The basis for relational self-esteem lies in our attachments to others, to whom we feel important just because we have a relationship with them (in other words, it is the relationship itself that is important). How much of your self-esteem today would you say is based in this idea of mutual attachment—of being important to someone not because of your position or your assets, but because you are attached to each other? To whom in your life are you attached? How many of these people are men? How much time do you spend with them?

In working on the above personal inventory, some men have found it useful to begin a journal. Indeed, this may be useful for several of the exercises that will follow in subsequent chapters. Keeping a journal has several advantages and can help you to get more out of this book. For one thing, it is a way of giving yourself time to stop and think. Being busy is too often an easy excuse that men use to avoid doing just that: thinking.

Another advantage of keeping a personal journal is that the act of writing puts some pressure on you to gather your thoughts and put them down in a way that enables you to share them better with others. Writing a book does much the same thing, and in ways this represents my own "journaling." I suggest you consider getting yourself a notebook of some sort at this point and using it as a combination diary/workbook as you go through the remainder of this book.

7

Adolescence

The Crucible of Identity

As boys approach adolescence, male identity development takes a decided turn. The approval and attachment dynamics and, consequently, the basis for both a positional and a relational identity continue to operate. At this point in life, though, males in our culture historically become increasingly aware of and concerned with establishing _differences_ between themselves and their peers. In other words, the positional orientation begins to dominate male consciousness. It would not have to be this way if the culture presented a more balanced view of masculinity, supported by a more balanced orientation toward self and others. As it is, however, the male search for identity turns into a search to establish a set of personal qualities (along with a set of personal goals) that are associated with competence and success, and therefore with recognition. These qualities and goals in turn become the foundation for male self-esteem.

The culture we live in plays a decisive role in the process of identity development. Through the mass media boys are bombarded with images of a masculinity that is based in relative position. These images are used to motivate them to desire various products from cigarettes to cars, all of which are carefully correlated with status and identity. At the same time, teenage boys borrow bits and pieces of their emerging identity from their fathers, often without acknowledgement or even awareness. For example, they often unconsciously associate themselves with their father's social position or income level, wanting many of the same things he wants. Many key attitudes toward work, authority, relationships, and self are also adopted from our fathers during adolescence. This typically goes on beneath a veneer of rebellion, which in boys reflects their ongoing need to be different from their erstwhile models and therefore individual. At heart, however, fathers and sons are cut from the same cloth much more than they might like to think.

As they start to construct the social world positionally, teenage boys begin to seek out a peer group that comes to symbolize their view of themselves and their perceived place in the world. The peer group becomes the crucible for the emergence of identity. The contemporary adolescent subculture is a tribal one that coexists with the adult culture but is also apart from it. Virtually every high school in America is organized socially along essentially tribal lines. In inner cities these tribes may coalesce into gangs; in the suburbs they sometimes include cults. Girls do this as well as boys, of course, but boys do it in their own way, based on power and status hierarchies. They focus on identifying ways in which their tribe (and, in turn, they themselves) are different from other tribes and individuals. The group becomes a clique, with many unwritten rules of conduct, a jargon of its own, and rites of initiation for would-be newcomers. It is bound together by a sense of alliance more than attachment, an egocentric and defensive stance that the male peer group takes toward the world at large. The process of gaining and maintaining acceptance into the peer group is no mean task; for some it is downright harrowing, whereas others find it a demoralizing experience.

Reflecting their awkwardness and anxiety in moving toward a positional orientation, adolescent boys as a rule are excessively rigid and preoccupied with their personal boundaries and their place within the peer group. At the same time, under the incessant barrage of advertising, possessions take on more and more connotations of status and position. Personal attire and appearance, as well as music and certain interests and activities (skiing, biking, skating, and so forth), become associated with place and identity. It is in this context of difference and relative position that the male sense of self takes form. As a rule, society expects teenage boys (and they expect themselves) to become increasingly competitive, self-controlled, resilient, and determined. One young man who was admitted to an adolescent substance abuse program that I started came to the admission interview wearing a T-shirt that said, "Only the tough survive." He struck me as a walking advertisement for the positional orientation to life.

Given the above scheme of things, it is not difficult to understand why adolescent boys would tend to abandon the relational orientation. On a personal level, becoming competitive and establishing a niche are much more compatible with detachment than they are with attachment. Socially, they are much more compatible with *banding* together than they are with *bonding* together. In order to develop any significant attachments and foster any kind of relational basis for identity and self-esteem, a boy at the least would have to have had such experiences before, and he would probably also need to have the relational orientation supported in an active way through at least one relationship with an adult male. This does not exactly describe a great many men I know. On the contrary, the following case is a good deal more typical.

The youngest of five children, Mark's parents divorced when he was four. He lived briefly with his father afterward but was soon sent to live with and be raised by a paternal aunt. She and her husband were kind and hardworking people who lived what Mark called a "no-frills life-style" in a small midwestern town. They tried to treat Mark fairly, even though they had two sons of their own and limited resources. In spite of these efforts, the emotional scars of Mark's early rejection never seemed to heal completely, and he was left with a lingering feeling of being "not quite good enough, not quite equal."

Mark had a hard time as a teenager. Having established weak attachments at best, he entered this phase of his life looking to create a niche for himself. As he surveyed the adolescent social scene, however, he did not seem to fit in anywhere. He did not much care for sports or for cars, yet he went to a high school where those were the main attractions. The vast majority of students had part-time jobs, and very few went on to college. What Mark liked best was to read, write, and draw, but these things were hardly important in the male hierarchy there. Therefore, even though these interests set him apart from his peers, they were not qualities he could build a masculine identity around. Although Mark was smart, the few "intellectuals" that attended school banded together on the basis of their higher social status, and he soon enough found himself left out in the cold.

Socially, as a result, he continued to live the more or less solitary life he had been living within his family. Adolescence only confirmed his identity as an outsider looking in, and it left him with a nagging feeling of inferiority.

Mark grew up to be a hard worker, but his insecurity followed him. Despite obvious intelligence, he had never had the confidence (or the resources) to pursue a higher education. So he had worked all of his life at jobs at which he excelled but that failed to challenge him. Because of his ability and his industriousness he advanced, becoming a manager of unskilled employees. He had a reputation, he said, for being a picky boss, but from his perspective all he was trying to do was to get people to do their jobs.

Mark married Denise, who herself was college educated and over the years had built a successful teaching career while she and Mark raised three daughters. Mark started drinking heavily after his last daughter was born. He was bored and frustrated with his life, lonely, and secretly envious of his wife's success and professional status. Within five years he was an alcoholic. He got sober by secretly going to AA, telling Denise only after he had been sober for two years. By the time he and Denise came to see me for marriage counseling, Mark had more than five years of uninterrupted sobriety behind him.

Denise described being married to Mark as "the best and worst" part of her life. On the one hand, he was a thoroughly responsible husband and a devoted father. He did more than his fair share of housework and child care. On the other hand, he was compulsive and controlling. As Denise put it, "There's two ways of doing things: Mark's way and the wrong way." Sound familiar? This is a modus operandi among insecure men. Needless to say, it had caused stress all through the marriage, and it had gotten worse rather than better over time.

Mark criticized Denise for virtually everything she did, from how she gave the kids baths to how she cooked and dressed. He even criticized the way she taught, although he had never set foot in her classroom! No matter what Denise did, it seemed, Mark could do it better, or so he seemed to think. He was forever interrupting to correct her and show her the "right" way to do something.

Mark also demanded a great deal of attention. He thought nothing of calling Denise up at work to talk about some bill that had to be paid or the chores that had to be done. He expected her to listen, and he would get angry if she said she had to go. In one of our sessions he defended this habit, saying, "I just want to talk to my wife. You'd think she'd be grateful. How many men think to call their wives at all? And all she wants to do is get off the phone. She never even tells me she loves me—just says good-bye and hangs up."

Mark could see nothing wrong in his behavior. He could not see, for example, how controlling he was. For a long time Denise had put up with it, consoling herself with thoughts that Mark's compulsiveness and criticism, his demands for attention, and his need to control everything were offset by his good qualities. Eventually, though, it got to her: one night, after he had ridiculed her housekeeping and parenting abilities over dinner with friends, Denise told Mark that he had better get help or else find someone else to kick around.

Asked what the major problem in their marriage was, Denise promptly replied, "Communication. We need to learn to communicate better." This has become quite a catchword in recent years. Everyone seems to agree that the problem is "communication," yet no two people seem to mean exactly the same thing when they use the word. With Mark and Denise, learning to communicate meant nothing less than him being able to confront, understand, and then work on overcoming his insecurity, to reassess his identity and his self-esteem, to establish relationships with men, and to redefine his marriage. Only then he was ready to "communicate" with Denise. Fortunately, both Mark and Denise were receptive to beginning our work by exploring Mark's history, labeling and understanding his insecurity, and establishing some personal goals as prerequisites to marital goals. Mark's openness to this process (he was, in fact, so burdened by loneliness and anxiety that he wanted to change) and Denise's patience were the conditions that made change possible for them.

Take a few moments to reflect on how your adolescent experience with peers, and specifically your experience in gaining acceptance into an adolescent "tribe," affected your self-image and the way you approached relationships. If you have begun keeping a journal, write down your thoughts in it. In particular, respond to these questions:

- Given your childhood experiences with adult males and the extent to which your early identity and self-esteem were based in approval versus attachment, what were you most concerned with as you entered adolescence? How concerned were you with finding your niche and with proving yourself in one way or another?

- What were the main tribes that inhabited your social world as an adolescent? What did you call them? How did they distinguish themselves from one another in terms of dress, language, or music? To what tribes were you most attracted?
- How successful were you at gaining admission into a peer group of your choice? What were the main things that brought this group together? What were the values and goals they stood for? Did you have any sense of real attachment to anyone in this group, or was it more a feeling of alliance (of banding together) that you experienced?

As the case of Mark illustrates, our experiences as adolescents with our peer group play an important role, just as our experiences with being valued as children do, in shaping our adult personalities. Equally important, they play a role in determining how we will approach relationships. The more insecure we are, the more difficult it will be for us to drop a positional orientation and open ourselves to attachment as a basis for identity and self-esteem.

Another experience associated with adolescence that also helps to shape men's lives has to do with their experience of first love. Concern over sexual desirability gets added to the complex mix of dimensions that boys use to begin constructing a competitive social hierarchy. Since men are socialized to view the world in terms of relative power, they also tend to equate power with sexual desirability. Therefore social status, athletic ability, intellectual ability, money, and possessions frequently overshadow relational factors (personal character, openness, respect, and so on) in a man's sense of his own sexual desirability. To be sure, adolescent boys are preoccupied with how they look, but they are also concerned with what abilities and other symbols of position they have. The more insecure he is, the more a man will take a positional approach to relationships. Of course, in order to reap the psychological and emotional benefits of relationships—namely, intimacy and bonding—he needs to do just the opposite.

A man's first falling-in-love experience, then, often says a great deal about his identity and his level of personal security. These experiences are revealing about the ways in which men go about getting the love they want, and about what their expectations are for what they will get out of relationships. The object of our first love says something about the relational life we expect to lead.

For example, Harry was a man with a heart of gold and a back of steel who always gave an honest day's work and earned a good wage in return, but who never was especially successful in his relationships. Actually, he considered himself something of a fool when it came to love. He was a big man, bearded and hairy. He worked alone much of the time, making good money as a skilled carpenter and cabinetmaker. He spoke in a soft and gentle voice that contrasted sharply with his rough demeanor. In his free time he liked to read and garden, and on occasion he tried his hand at poetry. When we met he was just getting through his second divorce. He had lost a lot materially in the process, but what was even worse for him was the sense of hopelessness that his second failed marriage had created. In his words, he thought of himself as a "born loser."

This was Harry's story of first love:

I guess I must have been sixteen, maybe seventeen. I was kind of a loner at the time. Actually, I still am. I spent most of my time alone then, and I still do. I have few friends. Never was any good at socializing; both my wives hated that. I'm just not good at talking. Better at writing, I think.

Anyway, about my "first love." I remember her, allright. Barbara was her name. Funny how we remember things like that. I actually only spent one day—one afternoon, really—with her. It was at a family picnic. She was a second cousin or something like that. I'd never met her before. Same age as me. From another state, though. She'd been visiting for a week, and was heading back the next day.

It's amazing, really, how little time we spent together. But I swear I fell in love with her. Head over heels in love. That doesn't seem like it ought to be possible, does it? But it happened.

I was awfully shy—just about as shy as I am today. But this girl, Barbara, she was friendly enough for both of us. Pretty, too. Bet I can still see her face if I close my eyes.

Anyway, she came right up to me and started talking. If she noticed my shyness, she didn't act like it. I remember being, well, intimidated by her looks. It made me nervous to look her in the eye. At the same time I couldn't stop looking at her face. God, I must have been a sight, staring at her like that, quaking in my boots! It was like I was in a trance. There was just something about her face, and the way she talked, that did that to me.

We ended up spending the afternoon together. We took a long walk together, and then I took her for a long cruise on the lake in my uncle's canoe. She sat up front with her back to me. Sometimes she talked or joked around, and sometimes she just sat there quietly. I remember staring at the back of her head, at her hair. It was long, light brown. I swear, I think I could have paddled Barbara around the world that day! Because she seemed to like me and not mind my shyness. And because she was so beautiful.

I never saw her again, and it took me a long time—believe me—to stop thinking about her all the time.

Harry was very much the same in his marriages as he had been that afternoon with Barbara. He worked hard and was a willing and generous provider; he was quiet and avoided arguments. So why did both of his wives leave him for other men? Was it because he chose untrustworthy women? Not at all.

In our work together, Harry came to see how his first love said a great deal about how he approached relationships. His afternoon with Barbara was an analogue for the way he was with women. On the one hand, he was a relatively quiet and uncomplaining provider. On the other hand, he also wanted very much to be in control. He was, to put it bluntly, both passive and stubbornly willful in ways. Not only did he avoid conflict, but also resisted compromise. He liked to think of himself as the kind of man who tried to be careful and fair; but in fact he often made his mind up quickly, and he rarely budged. He made a lot of decisions without talking about them first. He often preferred to do things himself rather than ask someone else for help. And he was very compulsive about how he ran his life, keeping everything in its place, making lists of everything that had to be done, and picking up after others even after they offered to do it.

Harry's first love also revealed the roles he expected himself and the woman in his life to play with regard to emotions. He was emotionally overcontrolled, and he had looked to his partners to bring feeling into his life. He also relied on them to be the communicators within the relationship. Both of his wives, he admitted, could probably have related to Barbara. Their personalities were similar; like her, they were much more emotionally open than he, and he described them as being generally happy people. Unfortunately, he joked, they had both gotten tired of being "paddled around" by him!

It took a while for Harry to see and then accept how he was in fact controlling in his relationships in this way, how he had relied on his wives to be his emotional side, and how they could have found that exasperating. Once he saw this, he wished he had seen it earlier. He knew he was shy and avoided conflict, he said. He thought it was this that had driven his wives to distraction. But he had not realized that he also expected to be the one in control, and for them to live his emotional life for him.

Time for male readers to get out their journals again. Take some time to think, and then write down your thoughts about the following questions.

- Can you remember your first love? Do you still remember her name? Can you picture her face?
- What did this first-love experience say about you and the way you are in relationships? What role do you tend to play, and what role do you (consciously or unconsciously) expect your partner to play?
- How do you expect to attract a partner? In other words, what about yourself do you think someone else would be attracted to? Yet another way to answer this is to think about what you have to offer in a relationship.
- How many of the things that you associate with being attractive have to do with status, power, money-earning capacity, or other aspects of your *position* in life, as opposed to personal qualities you possess or the way you relate to others?
- How many times has this same basic pattern, perhaps revealed in your first love, played itself out in your life?
- How do you exert, or try to exert, control in your relationships?
- To what extent have you looked to your partner to be the emotional and the communicative one in your relationships?

In the next chapters I will turn increasingly to the issue of building male self-esteem. I will look at a variety of issues that are seldom talked about by men, who have a tradition of equating self-esteem with competitive ability, with status, or with simple self-confidence. But self-confidence and status, as we all know, can be both elusive and unstable things. If they were the answers, then men with exceptional abilities would not be insecure, yet we know that there are many successful men who are severely insecure.

I hope that the material in this and the previous chapter has provided male readers with a clearer perspective on the forces that have shaped their own identity and formed the foundation for their self-esteem. Once formed, in my observation, a man's identity and the basis of his self-esteem remain remarkably refractory to change, unless he makes a purposeful and determined effort at it. Initially the pathway to change can be an upstream journey. Depending on how uncomfortable you are, and what your motivation for change is, it may be necessary to pursue some of the paths laid out here on simple faith for a while, at least until you begin to experience some of the benefits that change can bring. For this reason, it can be very helpful to approach this change process with other men. A professional counselor can also be helpful, but there is no substitute in my mind for the collective support of men who are willing to explore the possibilities of redefining masculinity, and to discover together what lies ahead.

8

Attachment and Identification

In his book *The Snow Leopard,* Peter Matthiessen relates the story of how he used hallucinogens for years in an effort "to fill a hollow place at the bottom of each breath."[65] I once had a patient—a young heroin addict who had never heard of, much less read, Matthiessen's book—who used very similar words to describe why he used heroin. I do not know precisely what hunger drove Matthiessen, but my patient's profound loneliness and sadness related in large part to his never having been able to discover who his parents were. Half Cherokee, he had always done miserably in school, except for one year when a teacher succeeded in igniting his interest in reading about Native Americans. On that single subject John was something of an expert.

These two men's common statement is one that, from my perspective, captures poignantly the emotional state associated with insecurity and troubled self-esteem. Matthiessen himself ultimately found self-acceptance not in drugs, but through a spiritual awakening that came in part through an arduous personal and physical journey. My patient found his, after many false starts, through Narcotics Anonymous.

Needless to say, self-esteem that is built on chemicals is not to be counted on when the chips are down. At best, chemicals can induce an transient euphoria or offer a brief flight into avoidance of pain and anxiety. Alcohol and other depressants, for example, can only suppress the pain of isolation for so long before those feelings begin to break through the surface of denial. Stimulants and narcotics can lead only to the most ephemeral state of bliss and self-acceptance.

Hallucinogens can create a curtain separating us from reality, but reality inevitably returns. Other addictions, from work to sex, function in much the same way.

Recovery from insecurity and recovery from addiction both begin when a man stops avoiding looking at his own wounds, when he stops trying to hide behind one obsession or another, and when he turns and faces his insecurity and isolation. Self-esteem, interestingly enough, seems to grow out of humility, or what Bill Wilson and the early founders of Alcoholics Anonymous were inclined to call *deflation*.[66] The profound insight that Wilson and his fellow alcoholics (and, apparently, Matthiessen) happened upon was that a man cannot build a totally satisfying foundation for self-esteem on competitiveness or achievement alone. Rather, they discovered that serenity and self-acceptance are found through humility and identification with others. Matthiessen's spiritual transformation came when he accepted with equanimity the fact that he might never spot the elusive snow leopard that was the object of his trek. This realization and its acceptance marked his departure from a strictly positional approach to self-esteem, wherein success is all that counts, toward one in which relationships also define the self. For Bill Wilson the turning point came when he embraced anonymity (as opposed to ego and individualism) as the spiritual foundation for a new way of life. For my patient, it came when he finally was able to accept that others could genuinely care about someone who felt anonymous.

The principles and traditions that guide the fellowship of Alcoholics Anonymous are enlightening with respect to how men need to redefine themselves and where they need to look for self-esteem. The traditions of AA specifically warn against the dangers of self-centeredness and a life run on willfulness and the need to be different. Keeping in mind that it was, after all, men who started AA, it is highly significant that in stark contrast to embracing an ideal based on competitiveness and radical individualism, AA advocates instead a primary commitment to the welfare and collective conscience of the *group* as the key to personal growth and serenity:

> For our group purpose there is but one ultimate authority—a loving God as he may express Himself in our group conscience.[67]

We believe that every A.A. group has a conscience. It is the collective conscience of its own membership. Daily experience informs and instructs this conscience. The group begins to recognize its own defects of character and, one by one, these are removed or lessened. As this process continues, the group becomes better able to receive right direction for its own affairs.[68]

The AA ethos is clearly more consistent with a relational than a positional orientation toward self and others. AA advises its members to pursue identification with one another and to surrender to the group conscience as the keys to living a sober life.

For those who continue to embrace the ethic of competition as though it were absolutely vital to psychological survival, it can be difficult, to say the least, to see how surrender and identification could possibly build self-esteem. When I talk to men about this idea, they sometimes question whether I am attacking their right to individuality, questioning the value of personal achievement, or both. Their attitude reveals just how completely committed they are to the idea that self-esteem must be based on difference and, by implication, *superiority*. To believe otherwise—and to give it a try—requires a leap of faith. That leap, however frightening it may be, offers the promises of nothing less than personal transformation and quantum change.

The position taken here is not that achievement, individualism, or competition are worthless, but that they at best represent only one pillar of identity—and you cannot build a very stable edifice on one pillar. I believe there can be no lasting self-esteem if the positional orientation that has dominated male identity is not balanced by a relational one. Just as there can be no such thing as true pride without true humility, so can there be no personal serenity if difference is not balanced by identification. Identification can indeed enhance self-esteem, as the following two anecdotes illustrate.

Ryan was a successful middle-aged executive when his career was suddenly cast adrift by a long recession and the subsequent downsizing of his company. One day he was making eighty thousand dollars a year, and the biggest issue he faced was trying to decide between either installing an in-ground swimming pool in his backyard or taking the family on a European vacation. The next day he was being interviewed at an outplacement firm that his company had hired as a consolation prize of sorts for the well-paid managers it was letting go, and being told that he might have to "adjust [his] financial targets." He felt his stomach sink at the sound of that particular euphemism for what used to be called "tightening your belt." As he drove home that afternoon, he felt a strange kind of disorientation settle over him. "It was like I knew where I was," he explained, "but suddenly I didn't know who I was. I knew my job was important to me, but it really stunned me to realize that it was that important, that I could actually feel like *nobody*. I understood then why some men kill themselves over things like that."

Ryan was able to maintain some semblance of optimism and to stave off the worst anxiety through the first three months of lonely and discouraging job hunting. After that, it seemed to get worse every day. When his wife finally could not keep up pretenses any longer and reluctantly brought up the subject of putting the house on the market, Ryan sank into a serious depression.

In all this time Ryan had essentially talked to no one, other than superficially, about his situation and how he felt about it. He shared some of his anxiety with his wife, but very little. He had also networked with a few men he knew, looking for job contacts, but he did not share his feelings with them either. Having based his self-esteem on his position, and his identity on his ability to compete, he found himself incapable of revealing his feelings of anxiety and his growing desperation. And Ryan sensed the distance in the men's voices he listened to over the phone, even as they offered words of support. Even the pair who met him for a drink after work seemed uncomfortable and eager to leave after half an hour.

Ryan came to see me on account of his depression. He confided that he had been thinking about suicide. At first they were only passing thoughts, but more recently he had found himself ruminating over it. I could well understand Ryan's depression, I told him. The cure for it, I suggested, would begin if and when he could bring himself to identify and join with other men. He seemed puzzled: wasn't there just some medication he could take? Yes, I replied, there were some that would help to mask his pain. But if he wanted a real solution for his depression, I suggested he try out a men's support group that I knew of. The group met twice a week and had been started by and for men who were out of work or anticipating being laid off.

Ryan turned pale, and his eyes grew large with genuine, undisguised fright. Then he frowned. I could see that my idea had not exactly lit a fire of enthusiasm. As it turned out, getting Ryan to go to a few meetings of this group was just about as difficult as getting an alcoholic to go to his first few AA meetings. He even used the same forms of denial to distance himself from "those people" (meaning the unemployed) whom he saw as somehow different from and inferior to himself. I asked him what his stereotype was about the kind of man who would go to such a group. He responded, after some hesitation, by drawing an image of a man who was the economic equivalent of the wino: basically a loser, someone who was chronically unemployed because of a character flaw, such as lack of ability or sheer laziness. I pointed out that this was once the dominant view of alcoholism—that alcoholics were losers, and that it was their own flawed character that was responsible. Again, Ryan seemed unmoved.

By persistently encouraging Ryan to keep an open mind and just to give my suggestion a try, I got him to agree to attend three meetings of the group. I asked him to do a lot of listening at these meetings, and to pay attention to any way in which he could identify with the experiences of any of the other men in the group. To his astonishment (though not to mine), he found that he did have something in common with at least some of these men. At first, I noticed, he was inclined to identify only with those men whose careers, education, and socioeconomic status were more or less similar to his own. I pointed this out and asked him to check out whether there were more fundamental ways in which he could identify with the other men in the group.

Three weeks later, Ryan came in and told me that he did not think he needed therapy any longer. "I realized what I was doing," he said. "I was really setting myself apart. I was trying to hold on to that idea of being 'different' and 'better than' that we talked about. Lately, though, I can see how I'm a lot more like all the other men in the group than I thought. It's just a matter of really listening to them and not denying the fact that I can relate. It's funny how I more or less chose who I wanted to listen to and identify with. If you hadn't pointed that out, I might have kept on denying my basic similarity to them forever. I feel really connected there now. That's where I want to get my support."

Before we parted I asked Ryan to tell me how it felt being able to identify with a diverse group of men. He described the experience using words like *comforting* and *empowering*. In a way that most men cannot understand so long as they choose to remain on the outside of the community of men (basing their identity and self-esteem on their position relative to one another), identification—dropping the desire to contrast in favor of the need to connect—does not lower self-esteem but actually enhances it.

The second man who had a powerful experience with identification was a therapist I knew who had devoted years of his life to becoming certified as a psychoanalyst and who prided himself on his credentials, his erudite understanding of the unconscious, and to a lesser degree, his cynical view of his fellow men. As much as I often enjoyed being with my friend because of his intelligence and humor, there were also times when his arrogance put me off. Sometimes I wondered if our relationship might be based more on some notion he had of us being a clique of two than on any genuine feeling he might have for me. He seemed so preoccupied with being superior that I felt uneasy, as though I could easily take a fall in his eyes.

I generally preferred not to argue much with my friend, and I had never brought up my occasional skepticism about his reasons for liking me. I also avoided talking to him about some experiences I had, for fear of taking that fall. But one time we were together and I let it slip that I had gone to some experiential men's workshops, including a few where I had participated in activities such as group drumming and dancing, as well as sitting in a tight circle with five other men in a white middle-class version of an American Indian sweat lodge. As I saw my friend's eyebrows slowly rise, I imagine he had something of the same reaction that Ryan did listening to me talk about the support group. Then my friend offered some rather unflattering interpretations of my behavior.

This time I was uncomfortable with my usual strategy of avoiding a fight, so I challenged him. "Why don't you try it out yourself," I suggested, "before you pass judgment on it." My friend looked startled, and he apologized. He had not meant to offend me, he said. I accepted his apology but must still have looked upset, for he leaned forward, caught my eye, and asked, "You really think I should do this?" I nodded.

Since my friend was in the habit of always doing things thoroughly, he did me one better and enrolled himself in a ten-day men's wilderness retreat. No sooner did I see him after his return than I realized he was a different person. I wish to make clear that I do not believe men's weekends (or even ten-day retreats) constitute the solution to men's problems of self-esteem or to their issues in relationships. Nevertheless, I do believe that my own experiences, like those of my friend, can represent at times what Robert Bly has called *openings*.[69] Such experiences give us a glimpse of what it could be like to relate to others in a different way. In my case (and, as it turned out, my friend's as well) it was the experience of identification and of a different way of orienting oneself to others that was the opening. For some people such openings can be the equivalent of spiritual awakenings and can lead to deep and lasting change; for others they simply do not.

The experiences that my friend described as most "opening" for him were those that involved group participation in activities like rites of initiation and—particularly interesting to me, because I could not imagine him doing it—dancing. He described one of his experiences this way:

> I had one experience in particular that affected me deeply. It happened on the morning of the third day. The group—there were about seventy of us—had decided to create a rite of initiation. I was sitting on the outside of the group, listening. Suddenly it hit me—I mean really hit me in a way that it never had before—that I was on the outside, and that I am always on the outside. I'm always keeping myself apart, I thought. I was sitting there, listening a lot less than I was analyzing, just like I always do. I'd been doing that for the first two days. Then I remembered your comment about experiencing something for myself before I judged it. That was the key word: *experiencing*. But that's exactly what I *don't* do. It's been my modus operandi. I've built an entire career on being detached, especially from men, I think. I don't experience. I observe. I measure. I especially measure myself in relation to other men.
>
> So I did something that was totally out of character for me. I got up and moved toward the center of the group. And it was funny, because it was as though the group sensed what I was doing. Some of the men looked up at me and smiled and moved over so that I could pass. Then a couple of them made a space for me on the ground up front. They spread their blanket so I could sit with them. It felt so good!

Then we did the rite. It wasn't complicated. Several men who were the drummers formed a line and started a beat—a deep, resonant one—and kept it going for nearly an hour. When one man would get tired he'd give his drum to someone else, who'd come and take his place in the line. We all stood and started dancing in place. Some men just jumped up and down and clapped their hands. Others really danced; I danced, too.

Then another group of men took off their shirts and lay down on their backs on top of a long row of blankets that some other guys had laid out. They formed two lines, head to head, with their arms up in the air. The way they were laying there reminded me of a long caterpillar, but with its legs in the air instead of on the ground.

Down at one end of this line, two men held a third man by his arms, turned him around, and then lowered him, back first, onto the outstretched hands. The caterpillar held him up and then passed him along in the air. When he got to the end, two more men helped him up. He clapped his hands and hooted, and everyone around him did the same. Then another man was let down onto the caterpillar, and the ritual was repeated.

It went on like that. My initial response to it was anxiety; it scared me somehow. But I watched it, and I cheered and hooted for every man who was passed along. I don't recall actually making a decision to place myself into the hands of the caterpillar. But at some point— just like when I got up and moved toward the center of the group—I walked toward the loading end of it.

There was one other man ahead of me. I watched him being lowered backward onto the upstretched arms. Hairy arms. Some were very muscular, others weren't. The faces of the men on the ground, the "body" of the caterpillar, were red. Their chests were sweaty. Considering no one had ever practiced, they worked in remarkable coordination to pass each man along.

Then it was my turn. The two men who were loading the caterpillar looked at me and smiled. I don't know if I smiled back. But I do remember thinking that I had no idea who these men were. I mean, I was aware that we had all dropped our usual identities. We were just men, together. Older and younger, heavy and thin, tall and short, bald and hairy—those were the main distinctions I noticed here. I'd come to notice what different men had to *say,* but I had absolutely no idea who they *were.*

Anyway, I went through with the rite of initiation. And you know what? It felt like exactly that: like I was being welcomed into the tribe. I was scared at first when those two guys turned me around and

leaned me over onto those hands. And then all of a sudden I was sus-
pended in midair. It felt incredible. I was floating on this sea of hands.
I closed my eyes. All I could hear was the heavy beating of the drums
and the clapping and hollering all around me. It was absolutely hyp-
notizing. I lost my sense of time. It couldn't have lasted more than
thirty seconds, but it felt like I was up there for a long time. Then I felt
two more hands take hold of my arms and lift me up.

I stood up and opened my eyes. Everyone was grinning at me, and
jumping up and down, hollering and shouting in joy. And you know
what? I felt proud.

The point of these stories is a simple one, and it is that identification, as opposed to comparison, leads to the development of attachment. Attachment in turn is a relational orientation to self and others. Experiences such as those that Ryan and my friend had led them
to see themselves in a profoundly different way than they were accustomed to. They were not used to identifying, and not surprisingly
they were not used to feeling attached to other men. Their "opening" experiences, however, allowed them to see (and define) themselves in relation to others. It was the similarities, not the differences,
that mattered.

These two men were opened to a relational orientation by placing
themselves in situations where they were stripped of their usual positional identities. In the support group and in the "tribe," respectively, Ryan and my friend were able to relate not so much through
the trappings of position as through the bond of manhood and
shared experience. Initially this aroused anxiety; in the end, however, both found themselves feeling very attached to other men for
the first time in their lives.

Identification and attachment, then, represent what could be
called one *relational pathway* to identity and self-esteem. By following this pathway, men can develop identities based not only on who
their credentials say they are and who they are in contrast to one
another, but on their feelings of connectedness and identification.
This approach to self does not negate credentials or abilities so much
as it adds to them another pillar for defining the self and self-worth.
In my experience this leads to a reduction of those feelings associated with insecurity, specifically the nagging anxiety and isolation
that so many men suffer from. It does not threaten individuality so
much as it provides a necessary context for it.

If you have been keeping a journal, take it out again and jot down some thoughts in response to the questions listed below. Once again I would urge men to explore the ideas and suggestions in this book not alone but together, through a support/growth group. Naturally there is a need for quiet contemplation, but there is also a need for sharing. Any man who reads this book and clings to the notion that he can overcome his insecurity alone is missing its most basic point.

Men tend to resist forming small groups whose primary purpose is communication and mutual support. A common defense is work: "I just don't have the time." Translated, this means that the idea arouses discomfort, or what Bergman has colorfully labeled "male relational dread."[70] Although Bergman identifies this anxiety as linked mainly to interactions between men and women, it has also applied in my experience to men's avoidance of intimate communication with other men.

By choosing work over the opportunity to communicate and connect with other men, we in effect affirm our choice of a positional as opposed to a relational orientation to life. Yet the great majority of men I speak to express a strong feeling of disconnectedness from other men. Many have never felt connected to or recognized their identification with their own fathers. Instead, they have separated themselves from other men, including their fathers, and have turned to women to affirm and even to define their masculinity. They may spend the bulk of their waking hours in the company of other men, yet never once form a true emotional bond with or feel attached to any of them.

Joining together with other men for the purpose of support, identification, exploration, and growth can open the door to a new way of defining yourself and your worth. By gradually letting down your barriers to identification with other men, you will in time discover what it means to become attached to men, to define who you are in part by those attachments, and to feel personal worth because of them. Here are some more questions that a group of men interested in exploring the relational orientation could spend some time thinking about and discussing.

- What basis have you used in order to identify with other men? To what extent have your friendships been more or less exclusively with men whose education, job, and social status are similar to your own? How do you feel when you are among men whose position in the world is very different from your own?

- How would you feel about the idea of forming a support/growth group where men would *not* be allowed to reveal what they did for a living, how much education they have, or where they live? This group would know each other only by first names, and communication would be limited to face-to-face or telephone conversations. How uncomfortable does that idea make you? What about it, do you think, makes you uncomfortable?

- How much are you able to see your father—including his attitudes, his values, and even his behavior—reflected in yourself?

- How difficult is it for you to be able to put yourself in another man's shoes, as the saying goes, and experience life from his perspective? What is the nature of any resistance you have to doing this?

- How do you react when another man gets very emotional, especially if he cries in your presence? Have you ever been with a man who was crying? What did you do?

- What experiences have you had that you think other men might have a hard time relating to (in other words, identifying with)? How would you expect them to react if you revealed these experiences? Suppose every man in a group writes down, anonymously, some personal experience that he thinks other men might have a hard time relating to. All the responses are then collected, shuffled, and passed out. Each man in the group takes a turn reading the experience that is handed to him, and then each man in the group makes a comment on how he would feel if that had happened to him. What do you think this experiment would be like?

- Think of two men you know who you identify with the most. How attached do you feel to them? Do you think they feel attached to you? Do you believe they would continue your relationship if you suddenly lost your job? Would you feel the same about them if they lost their jobs? What two things could you and these men do together that would lead you to identify with them even more?

These are only a few initial suggestions that can help a group of men get started on developing a relational orientation toward one another. At the same time, they are only a start. Men can be very creative (as my friend's experience with his rite of initiation showed) in finding ways to relate to and support one another as equals. I hope male readers will open themselves to this possibility.

9

Creating Culture

The current interest among some segments of the male population in recreating American Indian and other premodern, pre-Christian rites and rituals may well represent a reaction, just as Victorian romanticizing about relationships may have been in part a reaction to growing alienation between the sexes. In this case the reaction may be to a different kind of alienation, namely, the emergence of a generic global culture and the impending demise of true cultural diversity. If men are sensing on some level the loss of culture as a consequence of global economics—just as the Victorians may have sensed the loss of intimacy that gender divergence created—then their interest in symbols and mythical conceptions of masculinity, such as drumming and Jungian psychology, make sense if viewed as efforts to hold on to culture.

The ultimate purpose of culture, I think, is adaptation and socialization. Culture reflects the richly varied ways of living that people have developed over time to accommodate to different geographic locales. Culture, including its art, its technology, and its rituals, also represents a living metaphor for the group's relationship to its world. What I would call *endemic culture* seems always to be intimately tied to the land and to the process of socialization. Though books have recently been published on the subject of supposed cultural factors in family dynamics,[71] the larger reality is that mass media, global economic interdependence and competition, and technology have combined progressively to eliminate the influence of endemic culture and replace it with an increasingly dominant and generic global culture. Cross-cultural differences, in other words, are fast becoming much less significant than cross-cultural similarities. In order to experience anything close to endemic culture one has to travel great distances, and even then the culturally corrosive effects of technology and media are difficult to escape. Books like *Arctic Dreams*[72] and *The Snow Leopard*[73] tell us how difficult, if not impossible, is the search for unadulterated cultures—for groups that have not yet been co-opted by the global culture.

Culture can also be thought of as a template for living. It effectively sets the boundaries and expectations for relationships of man to woman, man to man, father to child, and man to community. It does this through its sex roles, rites, and traditions. Environment more than anything else may be primarily responsible for the diversity among endemic cultures ranging from the nomadic tribes of the American plains and the Arctic to the more or less implanted farmers of central Europe. Such factors as climate, soil quality, and the availability of resources for technology undoubtedly played a role not only in community survival, but in the evolution of spiritual philosophies, social organization, sex roles, and child-rearing practices. The richness and diversity of endemic cultures, however, has been largely replaced by a growing uniformity that reflects the spread of technology and the mass media. Signs of the global culture are everywhere. Modern cities look much more alike than different, and it is easy to find radios and televisions in even the remotest locales. The ethics of competition, acquisition, and consumption seem to thrive in virtually every nook and cranny of today's world.

My point here is that even as the smallest endemic culture affects its members on the level of relationships, spirituality, family structure, and personal values, so are all men today affected on all of these levels by the global culture. Two of the most basic elements of culture include an ethos (a position on man's relationship to and place in the world and the community) and a body of common wisdom or rules to live by. On a psychological level, self-esteem is linked in part to culture, for it is in the context of the cultural ethos and its common wisdom that men and women seek their identity. A crucial development stage for this process occurs in adolescence, as discussed earlier.

What messages does the global culture send to men about being a man and about their place in the world relative to one another? Very simply, it tells them that credentials, possessions, and status are the most important dimensions of identity and measures of personal worth. It tells them that competitiveness is the ultimate virtue, and that consumption and acquisition are proper ethics to live by. If this seems too cynical a view of the global culture, just peruse some of our most popular newsmagazines. You will find plenty of visual evidence of that culture—including ads for expensive cars, watches, perfume, clothing and so on—side by side with images of war, plague, and famine. This culture communicates a system of values that glorifies competition and position, at the expense of identification and relation, as the desired orientation to life. This orientation is increasingly influencing women as well as men. If men are to move beyond a positional orientation toward a more balanced one, they cannot afford to ignore culture. Given the current state of affairs, however, this means that we must be willing to preserve or even create at least some aspects of culture.

But can we create culture, or even parts of it? Can we possibly hope to swim against the increasingly powerful currents of the global culture? More pointedly, can we effectively teach values and ideas about a man's identity and place in the world that are at variance with the global ethos? I believe we can. But in doing so we must be careful to examine the messages about manhood that are communicated by our creations. It would be altogether too easy for us to create aspects of culture that unwittingly support position as opposed to relation as the sole basis for identity and self-esteem. This chapter explores some issues that men should consider in order to avoid doing just that.

Many rituals and traditions associated with endemic cultures have involved whole families and even whole communities. These traditions all share the same important social and psychological functions. For one thing, they affirm the worth of both the group and the individual. They also define both the position of the individual within the group and his relationship to it. Functional rituals and traditions create balance, giving each individual both a sense of place and a feeling of belonging. They make us feel a part of something larger, but also recognize us as individuals. In this context of functional culture, the individual can safely surrender to the group without losing his or her identity. In contrast, rituals and traditions that recognize only individual competitive ability drive the individual toward an unbalanced positional orientation.

The kind of rituals and traditions that men need to create for themselves (and their children), then, are those that honor the self *and* the self-in-relation. Such traditions and rituals enhance self-esteem and define the self in a balanced way. At the same time, they provide a counterbalancing influence against the selfishness and arrogance, as well as the underachievement and alienation, that so often come to dominate the human personality when it is allowed to develop under an ethos of competition and position. Unfortunately, many if not most of the rituals associated with the global culture celebrate individual achievement while largely ignoring the individual in relation to the group. The global value system is heavily slanted toward competitive ability as the basis for personal worth. Doubting their capacity to succeed in this system, young people are fleeing into underachievement and alienation in record numbers. Alternatively, they may embrace the ethic and become self-centered and grandiose. It is a major challenge for parents today to steer their children down some path between these two extremes.

The fabric of culture, then, is woven from ritual and tradition. Together they communicate our sense of place (our worth as individuals within a larger community) and the values we collectively live by. They balance individuality with community. To illustrate this, consider the following first-person account of an American Indian ritual called "sun dancing," written by a sixteen-year-old boy:

> This summer I pierced for the first time. As a young boy, I saw them sun dancing. It was so beautiful. I didn't understand it until later on. There was a real strong feeling between people, between different tribes. It was so good. I seen the men with their long hair flowing, the women in their buckskin dresses. It was so beautiful it made me weep. I wanted to be part of this. I wanted to feel this, spiritually and in my flesh.[74]

Sun dancing is an old and exceedingly complex tradition made up of many individual rituals and involving an entire community. Like virtually all such traditions, it is passed down orally and therefore is vulnerable to quick extinction if the endemic culture fails to remain intact. Such is the case with many modern and less complicated traditions as well. Can you think back to traditions within your own family that may have already fallen by the wayside simply because no one took the time to learn them, or took responsibility for continuing them?

Addiction, interestingly enough, is also associated with rituals. Particularly in the *habitual* phase[75] of substance abuse, drinking or using drugs becomes ritualized. Certain people, certain places, and certain routines become associated with getting high. This may be even more true for adolescent users than it is for adults. Once use becomes truly compulsive, rituals go out the window. The addict is preoccupied with getting high and loses his or her attachment to the rituals formerly associated with use. One teenage boy put it this way: "My group would meet at the same time, in the same place, every day. Now that I think about it, we'd all be wearing similar clothes, and our attitudes were pretty similar, too. I guess you could say that getting high was one thing—maybe the main thing—that my group existed for. It was the center of our being together, and it more or less bonded us to each other. There was a thrill to it, too. Until I lost control. Then I just got high all the time. It wasn't a thrill any more, it was a necessity."

Here is yet another account of an individual's response to encountering a functional culture. It is from the book *Narcotics Anonymous* and is aptly titled "An Indian Without a Tribe:"

> I went to a hospital in Louisiana and from there to a halfway house. This is where I found Narcotics Anonymous. N.A. was the tribe I never had. I found the same type of people that I had run with on the streets. There was something different about them. They had a peace I wanted.[76]

Although Narcotics Anonymous, like Alcoholics Anonymous before it, was started as a fellowship of addicts of addicts who banded together to help one another stay clean and sober, it has evolved into something akin to a culture—one that fills a need in the lives of recovering addicts like the young man described above. A careful reading of the explicit traditions that guide twelve-step fellowships,[77] as well as direct observation, through meetings, of the many that are not written, reveals them collectively to have struck that balance I speak of in terms of recognizing both the individual and the individual as he or she relates to the group. As models, these fellowships are worth the attention of men who want any culture they create to be functional.

Although the reader may consider the subject of this chapter somewhat abstract, in reality none of us can escape the influence of culture, or the need for it. If you doubt this, just consider for a moment the rise of cults and gangs that has taken place among adolescents in our society. I believe that the main factor responsible for this is the failure of the adult/parent generation to sustain a viable culture that includes their children. As a result the adolescent subculture has been allowed to exist outside the larger culture, developing its own ethos and rituals. These vary depending on the particular tribe that a modern adolescent joins; still, the culture inherent in contemporary adolescent peer groups is unmistakable. It includes an implied philosophy of life and a set of values, a style of dress and music, activities, and rituals. If adolescents today have a common problem, it is that they have been permitted to develop their own separate culture.

It is incumbent upon men, therefore, to create culture not only for themselves, but for their children. Men need not only to redefine masculinity, but to assume the responsibility for introducing their sons to culture and educating them in all of its intricacies. That culture, however, cannot be modeled primarily on the global culture I speak of here, with its glorification of competition and status. Too many young men cannot find a niche within this culture. At the same time, too many of their fathers are either casualties of it as well or else too caught up in it to devote enough time to their sons. Here is perhaps the greatest tragedy of a rigidly positional orientation to identity and self-esteem: that fathers and sons are competitive and detached from one another, when what sons need from their fathers is exactly the opposite (namely, collaboration and intimacy).

The exact content of rituals and traditions may be less important than their ability to achieve the needed balance between self and self-in-relation. One reason why some men today are looking to the distant past and to myth for solutions to their isolation and insecurity may be that they have abandoned or rejected the functional traditions and rituals from their own past, or else they were never exposed to them. One likely place to start looking for culture, then, is to do an inventory of your own past.

If you are a man, think back for a while on your own childhood and adolescence. If you have access to family photos, especially ones that were taken around holidays and family get-togethers, get them out and look through them. Then write in your journal (and share in your men's group) your thoughts about the following:

- What if any traditions did your family observe? Many of these may have been attached to religious or legal holidays: Christmas, Easter, Thanksgiving, Hanukkah, Passover, the Fourth of July, Memorial Day, Labor Day, and so on. Others may have been unique to your family.
- Traditions are typically supported by rituals. Thinking back on your family traditions, try to identify any rituals that were associated with them. What, for example, did your family do on these occasions? Did you have a meal together? Was anything *always* on the menu?
- Who seemed to be in charge of the action? In other words, who did the family rely on to set the stage, as it were, for the day's activities?
- As you reflect on your own family traditions, try to get in touch with how it felt to be there. Read the young Indian boy's account again, and listen to the feelings it evoked in him to be a part of the sun-dancing ritual.
- Did you ever participate in a religious rite or ritual, such as confirmation or bar mitzvah? As you look back on that experience, can you recall any feelings of being affirmed or recognized as an *individual* that you had at the time? Can you recall any feelings of being welcomed as a member of the *community*?
- Did your family have any daily or weekly rituals, such as Sunday (or daily) dinner together, saying prayers, or so on? What about such other rituals as decorating a Christmas tree, participating in a religious celebration together, or taking a vacation at a certain place? Again, how did it make you feel to anticipate such traditions? How did you feel when you were a part of it? Were your feelings about it different at different ages?
- What, if any, daily rituals did you create for yourself? Did you have any "habits" as a child or adolescent, such as saying certain prayers, saying goodnight to your parents, doing

certain things before going to bed, and so on? How would you have felt if you had not been able to follow your ritual?

- What, if anything, would you have changed about the rituals and traditions your family observed? What would you keep about them? Are there any traditions you would like to re-create in your own life?

Even people who grow up in so-called dysfunctional families can often get in touch with some feelings of warmth associated with being part of a tradition that defines a family's culture. Those who cannot do so may have had the misfortune of having no traditions— no family culture—to identify with, or they may still be too angry over past injuries to get in touch with any feelings other than resentment. Sadly, our current preoccupation with the dysfunctional family, combined with our growing alienation from traditional religion and the steady erosion of endemic culture, alienates more and more of us from whatever culture we were raised with. Some men are so bitter about their families, and often about religion too, that they find it difficult to identify anything good at all about these things. It is not my place to pass judgment about this, but I wonder whether they are not at times too blinded by their own resentment to separate what was good from what went wrong.

Whereas ritual and tradition bond us to the family and honor it, balancing self-interest with social interest, rejection of these things casts us adrift. In the cynicism that seems to define the times we live in, we continually uncover more and more forms of family pathology to feel ashamed of and to drive families apart with. As we fill ourselves with righteous indignation over a growing list of grievances, we leave behind an ever-widening wake of shattered families, discredited cultures, and individual "survivors" groping for safety.

Traditions and rituals not only provide us with a sense of place within the group and a recognition of our individual importance, but also communicate values. The Indian ritual of sun dancing communicates complex messages about the social expectations regarding men and women and the values that guide the community. Sun dancing honors men and women as individuals and in their relationship to one another, as well as the tribe and its relationship to the earth.

For the past half century those addicts who have been open to it have found strength and discovered a pathway to personal growth by *surrendering* themselves to a fellowship that believes first and foremost in a force that has capabilities exceeding individual willpower. This idea of surrender is beyond a doubt the greatest single obstacle standing between addicts and commitment to a fellowship that offers help and hope. It is no coincidence from my point of view that men should have started AA, the first of these groups, or that addicted men should balk at its most basic tenets. The philosophy underlying the recovery movement stands as a direct challenge to the ethic of radical individualism and the positional orientation to life. It asks us to place the welfare of the group over individual ambition (while respecting the integrity of the individual) and to subordinate competitiveness to a "group conscience," which is clearly a relational concept. Since men have been particularly vulnerable to addiction, as well as to isolation and insecurity, they would be well advised to give some serious thought to what the recovery movement is saying not only about addiction, but about being a man.

In trying to reduce their vulnerability to addiction, as well as in trying to reduce the feelings of isolation and insecurity that plague so many of us, men need to think seriously about the role that culture can play. In creating rituals and traditions, however, men are well advised to keep their eyes open. For one thing, they need to be careful not to create cultures that glorify competition and individuality over collaboration and community. They need to confront the fact that, in endemic cultures, acceptance of the idea of surrender is critical. No culture could exist if its members were to place individuality per se consistently over the group conscience, for this would lead inevitably to a radically positional orientation to self and others. It is also the basis, ultimately, for insecurity and isolation on a mass scale. By opting to define the self and self-esteem solely in terms of individuality, men have placed themselves in a situation in which competition drives them and where most of their psychic energy goes into maintaining their sense of relative position. By resisting the idea of surrender as much as we do, we perpetuate our own isolation and unhappiness.

Rituals can be as complex as the family Thanksgiving dinner, or as simple as a family having dinner together every night. They can involve a whole group, such as in a weekly family outing, or they can be such intimate one-to-one experiences as a father reading a bedtime story to his son. One of the great tragedies of our time is the progressive loss of small rituals among men and between fathers and sons. If you choose to work on this issue of creating culture, therefore, I suggest you postpone thinking about major rituals and focus instead on the smaller ones. Among themselves, men can create small but meaningful rituals that bond them, starting with something as simple as having breakfast together once a week. If you are a father, I would encourage you to initiate some small rituals between yourself and your child or children. A bedtime story or game playing is fine.

One word of caution, however: do *not* tie these rituals into either competition or behavior. If you play games, try to resist focusing on who wins so much as on the pleasure of being together. In a similar vein, do not make bedtime storytelling contingent on being a "good" boy or girl; use other rewards for that if you like. The focus of a ritual should be on merely being together, and on building a sense of attachment.

Through creative approaches to culture, men could establish a greater balance in the way they identify themselves and in how their sons define themselves. Positional values like competition, achievement, and acquisition could conceivably become balanced by relational values such as compassion, fairness, and altruism. Young men could then begin to seek self-esteem not only through being different from and better than others, but through being attached to and truly identified with others, including the community of men.

10

Collaboration
and Apprenticeship

The philosopher Hannah Arendt has argued that as men abandoned their communities and community-based occupations for cities and factories, entering the world of industrialization and mass production, they left behind a piece of their identities as men.[78] As modern life gradually stripped men of their ability to identify with and use the actual products of their labors, they gradually lost their connection to their culture. As if to fill the vacuum, mass marketing and advertising emerged, promoting an external sense of self based on possessions and status. This is the essence of the positional orientation toward self and others that has been described here. From this perspective, work is linked to identity and self-esteem through the credentials one has (degrees, certifications), the social status associated with one's work (professional versus nonprofessional, blue-collar versus white-collar), and the life-style one's income enables one to have. In modern societies, the actual products of men's labor may be of only marginal (or no) personal use to them; it is the *position* that work places them in that matters. They consequently are driven to preserve the life-style that is the foundation for their sense of who they are and what they are worth.

Work can and does contribute to a man's identity and self-esteem. But when it is rooted only in anonymous production, or when it is used simply as a means for acquiring possessions and a style of living that are symbols of position, it also leads to insecurity. Furthermore, it is isolating to the extent that men must be more and more competitive with one another in order to maintain and defend their life-styles. The pain of insecurity and isolation, in turn, promote addiction as a compensatory response.

Self-esteem that is based on acquisition and consumption instead of on production and conservation seems too often to end up as chronic dissatisfaction. Using work in this way as a basis for self-esteem proves to be ephemeral because it leads not to identification with what a person creates, but to an association of personal worth with what he or she has. Similarly, it leads men to establish only the most tenuous bonds with one another—bonds that are subject to being broken, as the following story illustrates.

Dave's forty-fifth birthday was barely a week behind him when he met with the manager of the computer division of the company he had worked for the past fifteen years. The manager said that in the most recent companywide comparative ranking of employees, Dave's performance had been rated as being somewhere between the fortieth and fiftieth percentiles. Dave felt his face grow hot as he listened. He knew what it meant—not only for raises but potentially for his job itself—to have more than half of the other employees in the company rated as better than him. Needless to say, he was crest-fallen. He had hated these comparative ratings, he told me. "All these ratings really amount to is a comparison of how many hours you're willing to put in, and whether you have any boundaries or priorities in your life at all."

Dave honestly felt that he was a good employee, conscientious and competent. He described himself as a self-starter and someone who really cared about the quality of what he did. In his early days with the company he had been generally regarded as a rising star. So, I asked, what had happened? How did he account for this disappointing rating?

Dave was of the opinion that two things were going against him. The first, he said, was his age. He had no doubt, although he felt the company would surely deny it, that there was a strong correlation between age and ratings. The highest ratings would be found to cluster around employees younger than him. They would almost all be men, of a type known within the organization as "drivers" (a tag referring to the fact that these were young men who lived and breathed work). "They're ambitious and competitive as hell," Dave explained. "They spend their time literally trying to outdo each other in how many hours they can work. We hardly get the chance to get the bugs out of a system anymore before they're out there busting their chops trying to replace it with a new one. It's pretty obvious to me that this is a game they're playing: who can be the smartest. And what really gets to me is that they pretend to be so friendly and buddy-buddy with each other, when it's so obvious that they can't all be winners. It's all an act. After all, the company ranks us in comparison to each other, right? And there can't be two number ones."

The situation had been similar, Dave admitted, back when he was a rising star, but with a couple of differences: "These new guys make the 'company men' of my day seem lazy by comparison. And at least we sometimes worked together. I'm telling you, any semblance of cooperation between these guys is strictly for show."

Aside from being middle-aged and more interested in getting an existing system working right than in installing the next generation, Dave felt that he had something else going against him: He was not ambitious enough, at least not in comparison to the drivers. Though he did his job and did it well, he was not especially interested in moving up any more. He would much prefer to really be part of a team effort now, he said, and share equally in whatever success the team achieved. He was not averse to working hard, but he did not see the need to work ten-hour days and come in on weekends if he did not absolutely have to. But he had known for a long time that the corporate culture in his firm was organized into two groups: the drivers, who were on the way up (and who knew no limits), and those who were euphemistically referred to as the "RIP's", with the initials standing for "retired in place." If you were not a driver, it seemed to Dave, you were somehow suspected of being deadwood. "It almost doesn't matter if you do your job well, if you've been a loyal employee as I have, or if you've got the company's best interests at heart," he explained. "It's more like you're either superambitious, workaholic, and cutthroat competitive, or else you're an also-ran and very possibly on your way out."

I asked Dave what he could do about this situation. "Well," he replied, "my boss told me that he'd go to bat for me over it. But to tell you the truth, I don't believe him. He's a nice enough guy, but I don't think there's a damned thing he can do about the way the company operates. He wants to keep his job, too, and he's not going to go to the higher-ups and tell them the system stinks."

Dave was caught up in a situation that is familiar to most men I know. He was anxious, depressed, confused, and filled with self-doubt. In large part his sense of who he was, along with his self-worth, had been connected for as long as he could remember to his job and his position. His comfortable suburban life-style represented tangible proof of those things. Moreover, as his recent experience at work confirmed, any effort on his part to balance work with family life—to set limits on work—would very likely have negative consequences. To a degree he could not help but feel guilty about not wanting to be a driver, even though another part of him sensed that it would lead to unhappiness of a different kind.

Dave's dilemma was not easy to solve. We both knew that he would probably have to make some compromises. He did not want to lose his job and his life-style in order to protest the corporate ethos, but he wanted to continue to pursue what he called greater "balance" in his life. Together we worked on these goals.

Using work as a basis for self-esteem—as either a symbol of personal worth or a means of earning money to purchase other symbols—is, of course, consistent with the positional orientation that men have been socialized to take. From this perspective, it is one's status in the workplace that represents one brick in the wall of self-esteem. I have no case against using work in this way, but I see clear problems when men's self-esteem becomes overly dependent on it.

It is also possible to approach work and its place in men's identity and self-esteem from a *relational* perspective. Two relational pathways to self-esteem that involve work are collaboration and apprenticeship. I will examine each of these and illustrate how men might move in these directions.

In order to build self-esteem through work, it is an advantage if a man can identify himself with the products of that work. As managers of mass-production manufacturing plants know only too well by now, the detached worker is a sloppy, unmotivated, even angry worker.

A simple example of identification with work is the carpenter, jeweler, or cabinetmaker who stamps his mark into his work. Another is the man who makes something for his own personal use and thereafter keeps, maintains, and repairs it—usually much sooner than he would discard or replace it with something newer. One man I knew felt this way about his garden, another experienced it through the pottery he created, and a third was an accomplished carpenter in his spare time. Perhaps there are things you create, or interests you have, that you identify with as well.

Although these are all examples of individual work, they suggest that it is possible for a man to develop a sense of relationship with the fruits of his labor. This relationship, like the attachment that can develop between men through identification, can be unconditional and noncompetitive. It can be based not so much on one's work being better than what other men do, but on identifying with that work as a reflection of yourself. To do this we need merely to take away the need to use work as yet another way of standing apart from others; then work can become collaborative and still feed each individual's self-esteem.

Some contemporary subcultures, such as the Amish in Lancaster County, Pennsylvania, continue to maintain a tradition of collaborative work in which all who contribute share in the benefits, the satisfaction, and the self-esteem that comes from identifying with what one creates. Habitat for Humanity which similarly emphasizes collaboration in the building and repair of homes, is another example. The focus is not on what the work can get you or how well you are doing in comparison to someone else; rather, it is on what you do *collectively*. Naturally, a job that is done well boosts self-esteem more than one that is not, yet the latter seems rarely to happen in such situations. Rather, collective skill, like "group conscience" in AA, seems to prevail. Pride then becomes something that can be shared, and that the individual does not experience at the expense of others.

Some of the more obvious forms of collaborative work that meet the essential requirements for building self-esteem include growing things and building things. Collective community service might also qualify. I suggest you pause to think (and write, if you are keeping a journal) about this notion of collaborative work. Specifically, what if any experiences have you had with it? What role does it play in your life today? Can you foresee ways for collaboration to play a larger role in your self-esteem? To stimulate your thinking, the following is a personal account of one of my own experiences with collaborative work.

Because my father was an executive, my family moved a number of times while I was growing up. When I was around fifteen, we moved from the relatively rural environment of a small city in up-state New York to densely populated suburban Long Island. We had lived there before, and though I had much preferred the small-town atmosphere I can not say our new home was altogether unfamiliar terrain, geographically or socially.

We moved into one of a small group of new, slightly upscale homes that had been built in a neighborhood of older and somewhat more modest houses. Our houses were all raised ranches; theirs were traditional Cape Cods. From the beginning it was obvious that all of us in our minidevelopment were less than welcome. My father said it was because we lived in newer, nicer homes, but I thought it was because our houses had taken up the last bit of open space around.

Our little group of families had significant differences in terms of what the men did for a living and therefore the expectations that each family had. Our family almost knew we would be moving again; others almost knew they would not be. My father was a busi-nessman; the man next door was a union official; and the man next door to him was a salesman. Despite these differences in social/occu-pational class, we all became good friends, establishing our own subculture of sorts amid the "old-timers" across the street. Those families, although separated from us by no more than forty feet of sidewalk and asphalt, remained something akin to foreigners. I so-cialized almost exclusively with kids from my side of the street (who were few), plus some friends I made at school. At best I enjoyed cordial, though never close, relations with the boys across the street.

One Saturday morning in May, I woke to the sound of men's voices in our back yard. This was not an expansive space, to say the least. All six homes in our minidevelopment had been built on the 60-foot-by-100-foot lots that met the minimum zoning require-ments. Altogether they spanned 360 feet of frontage. The back, meanwhile, overlooked a substation of the local power company—a neat but singularly ugly composition of large boxy transformers, is-lands of concrete, seas of gravel, and a myriad of wires, insulators, and towers that looked as though they had been made from a giant erector set. All of this was enclosed within an 8-foot-high cyclone fence topped by three strands of barbed wire; the wire sagged badly in many places where it had been climbed over repeatedly to retrieve errant baseballs, footballs, rockets, and kites. The utility company had planted some evergreens around the perimeter, about half of which were dead brown. Everyone in the development agreed that it was an eyesore.

The deep, resonant rumbling sound of all those men's voices drew me instantly out of bed. I had never heard a sound quite like it before. I went into the bathroom, looked out the window, and saw my father and all the other fathers from our side of the street standing in a group in the middle of our back yard. They were talking animatedly, and one of them (who was actually the grandfather of one of my friends) repeatedly pointed toward the substation while making sweeping gestures with his other hand. Whenever he would do that, the rest of the group would momentarily stop talking and look in the direction he was pointing. Then they would nod and start talking again.

My curiosity piqued, I threw my clothes on and padded on down. As I approached the group, my father looked over and briefly caught my eye. As was his custom, he neither smiled at me nor said hello, but some slight change in his expression registered in me as recognition and acceptance. I took a place at the outside of the circle and listened attentively.

I soon discovered that there were two topics being discussed. The first, as usual, was the substation and its ugliness. The other topic was a collective venture in fence building. After several informal meetings, the group had decided that what our minidevelopment needed was a good fence between us and the substation. The consensus was that a tall, solid wood fence would at the very least provide some visual relief from the dreaded sight. It might also, one man said, protect our property values.

The actual work itself was being planned that very moment. It was to be a joint effort, with everyone contributing both money and effort. I knew intuitively that I would be doing some of the work, and the idea excited me.

It took us a full month of weekends to build the fence. At times as many as nine of us—four fathers, a grandfather, and two uncles, plus myself and one other adolescent—worked on it at once. When finished, the fence was 6 feet high and 360 feet long. It was hard work, but feeling a part of this team effort, I voiced no complaints. I did what I was asked to do, from digging holes to holding boards being sawed or nailed into place to staining and varnishing the whole fence to protect it from the weather. Everyone worked hard.

The men sweated, alternately cursed and laughed together, and treated me like I was one of them. At the end of each Sunday, the men drank beers and talked about what was to be done next. I stood around and reveled in our creation.

Years later, the fence was something that the men on our side of the street still talked about at times. Of course, it did not entirely blot out the substation. Eventually the power company planted new shrubs (which lived), along with some small trees (half of which died). My family eventually moved, though we stayed a lot longer than I would have predicted. My parents kept in touch with the neighbors, all of whom did stay. Once, after we had been gone for a number of years and I was finished with college, I found myself in the area of my old neighborhood and took a short detour, just to look at the fence. It had aged and badly needed repairs in places, plus a new coating of stain. But it was still there. I stood staring at it for a moment, and could still feel the satisfaction.

Depending on just how competitive you are, and how much you have come to define yourself on the basis of being different from and better than other men, you may resist this idea of collaborative work. Typically, men's resistance to it takes one of two forms. First, there are those men who simply *have* to be in charge. Their identity and self-esteem cannot make room for the notion of a group conscience or true collaboration. They build their own fences, and then compare them to those built by others. These men are usually the most insecure and isolated of all. They are the most entrenched in a positional orientation to life. As a rule they have few close friends, and those they do have are mostly connected through work in one way or another.

A variation on the above is the man who is willing to collaborate, but who believes that some men are "more equal" than others. They may be able to work alongside others and to compromise, but they instinctively move toward breaking up a group into cliques. In effect they can not help making every situation into a competitive one, organizing every group of men into a totem pole and placing themselves somewhere on it (usually near the top). These men have one advantage, which is that they can come to feel attached to at least some men in a group. What they need to do, of course, is to take the next step: to identify with *all* men in the group, and to stop comparing themselves to others all the time.

I would encourage men's groups who wish to work together on building self-esteem to move beyond talking (as important as that is) to the level of collaborative work. Choose a group or a community project, make a collective commitment, and do it. The outcome of this collaborative effort needs to be a collective product—something that all can feel identified with and proud of.

Another form of collaboration that is available to men, but rarely taken advantage of any more, is parenting. Whereas many women still do at least some collaborative parenting, men do hardly any. I am talking about things like active participation (along with other men) in day care and school programs, group father-son camping trips, and even such simpler activities as spending an afternoon together in a local park. Again, competitive sports can be fun, and can even be an arena for learning certain values like fairness, but beware of the tendency for competition to foster a positional orientation. If competition is somehow allowed to become the focus of these collaborative activities, do not be surprised if at least some of the children opt out. If collaboration is truly the focus, however, the children will most likely get more and more involved over time.

Apprenticeship is an exceedingly old social institution. The root meaning of the word is "to learn"; significantly, it also has relational connotations. The apprentice and his teacher (or master) traditionally had a relationship that demanded mutual respect, and which lasted a relatively long time. As the apprentice would one day inherit the master's shoes as it were, the relationship was hardly a detached one; on the contrary, it was quite involved. The apprentice learned his art, trade, or profession as much, if not more, through informal talk and modeling as he did through reading and formal instruction. It could also be argued that the master had as much at stake in the relationship as the apprentice, since the work of the latter reflected on the former.

The modern equivalent of the apprentice is the trainee, although in light of the perspective presented here, the two are not really equivalent at all. The very word *trainee* connotes position, not relationship—and a very lowly one at that. As anyone who has ever held that title knows, there is nothing lower than a trainee. The trainee does not have a master so much as he or she may have a supervisor or trainer. Though there may be some investment in the relationship, it hardly connotes either the same level of involvement or investment as the apprentice-master relationship.

The above is more than a matter of semantics. The words we use to describe relationships reveal a great deal about their role in our lives and how we use them to define ourselves. Trainees are fairly anonymous; apprentices are not. Apprentices work under their masters for long periods of time, learning many aspects of a trade or skill. Trainees come and go. Being an apprentice implies a relationship; being a trainee does not.

So although the concept of the trainee fits in nicely with a positional orientation to life, the concept of apprenticeship is much more compatible with a relational view. It is through the latter that men can simultaneously learn things and build their self-esteem by establishing connections to others. The master-apprentice relationship is the relational connection that makes this possible.

Before going on, male readers should take a few minutes to do some journal writing around the following questions. If you have formed a men's growth group, discuss these issues with one another after you have had a chance to think about them individually.

- How well do you relate to this notion of apprentice versus trainee? Can you get a feeling for what it would be like to be in each of these roles? Imagine yourself, for a moment, being a trainee. Imagine what your relationship with your trainer is like. How do you feel in that relationship? Do you feel attached to your trainer? Do you have a feeling that your trainer is attached to you? Do you feel that you each have a personal investment in the relationship? Do you feel that you personally matter to the trainer? Does he matter to you? Does this relationship feel like it will last for a long time?
- Now switch gears and try to imagine yourself as an apprentice. What skill or trade would you be learning? Imagine your relationship with your master. What is this relationship like? Is it an important relationship for you? Is it important to him? Can you imagine it lasting for a long time?

One of the key questions above has to do with what you imagine yourself learning from your master. Equally important, however, is the issue of the relationship itself and how it makes each person feel about themselves. Both the master and the apprentice derive self-esteem from their relationship in ways that a trainee and trainer cannot. If you doubt this after thinking and talking about the above questions, then you may need to experience the real thing before you will be convinced. That would mean being willing to become an apprentice of some kind.

This could be considered an experiment in personal growth, but it could hardly be considered an "exercise," simply because the apprentice-master relationship needs time to develop. Attachments do not come from brief exercises or transient gatherings; they emerge from relationships. Some of the saddest accounts I have heard have come from men who sought attachments to other men in weekend or weeklong workshops. Many did experience some sense of bonding, only to have it replaced by a hollow loneliness when the gathering ended and everyone went their separate ways. Back in the 1970s, many people had similar experiences with what were then called "encounter groups." From the present perspective, the encounter-group movement emerged in response to the chronic alienation that living in a mobile, competitive society creates. These are desperate efforts at best, and they are not a pathway that I would advocate for men to follow.

In order to experience the self-esteem that can come from an apprentice-master relationship, you really have to make a commitment to it. I would recommend at least a year. Naturally that means being thoughtful about what you do before you do it, including giving some thought and doing as much talking as you can about what you would like to learn. It also means thinking about and selecting an appropriate master who will teach you and also be willing to engage you in a relationship. It is not inappropriate for this to be a formal, paid relationship, especially if what the master teaches the apprentice can at some point be used by the apprentice to earn money. Alternatively, some form of barter system could be established to create a sense of equity in what the apprentice and master each get in addition to the relationship itself. This is not intended to reduce the relationship to a mercenary level, or even to minimize the importance of the relationship. On the contrary, once equity is established, the relationship can grow.

Selecting a master is probably best done in collaboration with other men and the potential master. You will need to think about the personal qualities you would look for in someone you were to commit yourself to for a minimum of one year. This person will also have to be expert enough in the skill or trade you want to learn to command your respect for their ability. Do not, however, make this decision solely on the basis of the master's competitive reputation. Examine the actual work that this person does, and talk with him to get a feeling for what it would be like to be in a relationship with him. Finally, decide in advance just how much time you will devote to being an apprentice, preferably on a weekly basis, and also get a commitment from the potential master about how much time he will be willing to commit to you.

In thinking about becoming an apprentice, let your creative side go. Forming a growth group and using it as a "think tank" can be very helpful in this process. Most men do have some secret desire to learn one thing or another, from carpentry to mountain climbing to pottery making. What would you like to learn?

Becoming an apprentice is one way to pursue identity and self-esteem through work via a relational pathway. Another is through being a master to someone else. Unfortunately, both mastering and apprenticing are largely lost social institutions. In writing about them here, I realize that in many ways I am asking men to pull themselves up by their own bootstraps. But this may be a reality we simply can not escape, and it need not be one that stops us. Again, I believe that the best insurance for these efforts succeeding is through forming a men's growth group and learning increasingly to trust the group conscience by talking, listening, and following consensual advice. This process, which assumes that the individual will take a back seat at times to the wisdom of the group, will not only facilitate the apprentice-master relationship but lead to the development of mutual attachments among the group members. In this way, the growth group itself becomes a relational pathway to identity and self-esteem.

Being a master means, among other things, being willing to make a commitment to a relationship with another man. Think about that. If the idea makes you uncomfortable, that is not unusual. Talk about it with other men until you begin to feel more comfortable with it. Answer these questions for yourself:

- What would you be worried about if you were to make a commitment to work with another man for at least a year? What problems could you foresee happening?

- In what areas would you feel comfortable being a master? What would you want in exchange for your efforts?
- How much time would you be willing to commit to your apprentice? What conflict might this create in your own life, and how would you resolve them?

Aside from serving as a master to another man, men can help both themselves and the next generation by being willing to enter into similar relationships with their own sons and/or with other youths. Too many men have had experiences like Russell's:

My father was a self-taught carpenter. I don't know exactly how he learned it, but he could and did make almost anything out of wood. Not just bookcases, but tables, dressers, even chairs. I'd help him out sometimes, but that became so uncomfortable that I eventually gave up. He expected me to know what I was doing without having to learn it. He was very critical, and often impatient with me. It didn't boost my confidence at all. On the contrary, it made me avoid trying to fix even a broken shelf when I was an adult.

The above is a good example of how the father-son relationship in our society has deteriorated from what could be described as a mentoring one to a competitive one. I have heard similar sentiments repeated countless times. Think back on your relationship with your father. What, if anything, did he know how to do that you would have wanted to learn? Did you watch him? Did you help him? What was his attitude toward you? If you had a positive, mentorlike relationship with your father, consider yourself one of the lucky few and try to pass that experience on down to either your own son or some other young man.

Mentoring one's own child seems like a natural thing for a father to do. Naturally there may be interests that a child has on which we cannot mentor them; in that case, we help them best by helping them find an appropriate teacher. But there most likely will be at least some skills we have that our sons may want to learn. When we respond to their interest with impatience, and when we deny them the opportunity to learn from trial and error, we undermine their sense of who they are and of their worth.

I would encourage men to explore the possibilities of mentoring youths collaboratively. Rather than going it alone, use the growth group as a vehicle for supporting and guiding each other's efforts. If you find it difficult mentoring your own son, use the group to help you solve the problems. Try mentoring another group member's son. Keep in mind that the same master-apprentice ground rules apply: this is a commitment of relatively long duration; there needs to be some fair exchange; and this youth and yourself will most likely come to feel attached to one another.

If men are to overcome the deep feelings of isolation and insecurity that are so pervasive among them, and if they are to reduce their vulnerability to addiction, they vitally need to reclaim their roles as fathers/mentors. It makes no sense to me that they try doing this without the support of other men, or that they look for it in brief encounters rather than through committed and involved relationships with one another and their children.

This second part of the book has outlined what could be thought of as a series of relational pathways to self-esteem. By pursuing them, I believe that men could in time learn not so much to abandon the positional orientation to self and others, but rather to balance it with a relational one. This will more likely be a slow but steady as opposed to a fast or dramatic process. Although we may now and then achieve an important insight through an "opening" experience of some sort, we need to be prepared to do the longer, harder work of being with one another, of risking becoming attached to one another, and of learning to entrust ourselves (at least at times) to the higher and loving power of the group conscience.

PART THREE

Men and Intimacy

After lust gets underway, it is extremely powerful. In fact, if one over-looks his experience with loneliness, he may well think that lust is the most powerful dynamism in interpersonal relations.

—*Harry Stack Sullivan*[79]

11

Male Intimacy and the
Disenfranchised Self

With the statement that opens this last part of the book, the neo-Freudian psychoanalyst Harry Stack Sullivan laid the foundation for what he called the *interpersonal* theory of psychiatry,[80] elements of which have reappeared recently in what has been called the *relational* view of psychological development.[81] Both Sullivan and those associated with the modern *self-in-relation* school believe that psychological development takes place (or fails to take place) in the context of relationships. This remarkably simple notion actually contrasts sharply with more traditional psychodynamic theories of development that place more emphasis on processes within the individual than on attachments or other qualities of relationships. Both the interpersonal and the relational views are founded on the idea, implied more than directly stated in Sullivan's comment, that the desire for interpersonal connectedness is the fundamental human drive and is critical to understanding psychological development and pathology.

I believe, as Sullivan suggests, that loneliness is in fact a much more aversive state than sexual deprivation and that the desire for interpersonal connection is in fact more primary than the sex drive, although the latter, thanks in part to Victorians like Freud, has gotten much more attention.

According to interpersonal theory, psychological development proceeds in a relational context (though Sullivan typically places undue emphasis on the *mother*-child relationship) and leads to the development of three parts of the personality: the good-me, the bad-me, and the not-me. I believe the last of these has the strongest implications for men's problems of intimacy. I prefer to call this aspect of the self the *disenfranchised self,* since it contains all those aspects of personality and experience that the individual chooses not to acknowledge or legitimize simply because they are not a part of the identity he or she has been socialized to develop.

Like Alfred Adler, whose comment marked the opening of the second part of this book, Sullivan implies in his writings that he is describing the development and pathology of both men and women. As one reads his work in detail, however, it appears that, like Adler, Sullivan describes the experience of men in particular. Though women may relate to his descriptions, it strikes me that he describes best how men have been socialized in a way that maximizes their isolation and creates insecurity. Their positional orientation, and the concept of masculinity that has evolved from it, creates a disenfranchised self that renders men vulnerable to feeling isolated and insecure.

What is in the disenfranchised self? Very simply, it is made up of all those experiences that are not acceptable to men as part of their identity. This includes every emotion and thought that is not consistent with being competitive, self-controlled, and resilient: feelings of vulnerability, the need for connection, the desire to be nurtured and comforted, and so forth. At best, men are ambivalent about having such thoughts and feelings, as well as about revealing them. The more insecure they are, the more their ambivalence turns to fear and then rejection of parts of the self, to the point of repressing their own thoughts and feelings. At this extreme, men are left with no option other than to lead vicarious emotional lives—to try to manipulate others to do much of their feeling for them.

Our tradition of gender divergence lies at the heart of the disenfranchised self. Clearly women have such aspects of their selves as well, though the focus here is on how this concept applies to men. Starting as soon as a boy becomes aware of sex-role differences (which is usually somewhere between the ages of five and seven), his identity begins to evolve into a self that is enfranchised and one that is not. I have already discussed those qualities that have been associated with masculinity for the past two centuries. These are part of the enfranchised self for virtually all men, and they include such qualities of personality as emotional self-control, strength and perseverance, a concern for objective rules and boundaries, and competitiveness. Men and masculinity have been associated with being "in the world": tough, a provider and/or protector, and worldly or streetwise. You can observe even young boys as they begin to conceal or minimize their own anxiety, vulnerability, or need for comfort and to detach emotionally rather than share their pain or distress with their mothers or fathers. Boys learn at an early age to become stress absorbers.

Ingrained social traditions of gender divergence plus a boy's modeling of his father (or some substitute) lead to his increasing tendency to disenfranchise aspects of his self. This leads to identity development and individuation, but also to a separation and a loss of connection that mothers are usually the first to feel. Since emotional restraint is part of the masculine identity, boys typically do not turn to their relationships with their fathers as substitute outlets for intimacy. Instead, they begin the process that leads them down the path to chronic loneliness, isolation, and anxiety. To escape their distress, men in vast numbers have turned to alcohol, drugs, sex, and work for comfort.

Here is a story that many women readers will find familiar. A husband comes home from what his wife assumes is at least as hard a day at work as she has endured. Anxiously awaiting his return and eager to connect, she watches him as he throws his coat on a hanger, flops into a chair, and sighs heavily. "How was your day?" she asks. "Okay," he replies, his face tense. "What happened?" she asks. "Nothing," he replies, whereupon she feels disappointed if not downright frustrated. Her options then are to tell him about her day (and perhaps suffer his bored expression) or else turn her attention to something else.

Women have a hard time understanding this very typical interaction. They conclude that the man in their life thinks too little of them to bother to share his daily experiences, is angry or upset with them, regards them as unsupportive, or some combination of these. Some accept this as a part of their partner's personality, though they are becoming more and more of a minority. Many more women are getting angry and demanding communication.

The question that plagues these women, of course, is *why* their partners choose not to communicate with them. If pressed to communicate these men will get irritable, and if pursued enough they may get angry. As baffling (yet generic) as this kind of interaction is, its explanation is actually not complex. To understand it, one has merely to understand the male and female sex roles as they evolved under the influence of gender divergence and appreciate the psychological implications of the Victorian concept of masculinity that lingers on to this day.

From that perspective, our hypothetical husband is simply being a typical man. Accustomed to being a stress absorber and to dealing with anxiety by himself, he may not want to upset his wife or act in ways that run contrary to his image of himself by telling her about the disappointments, frustrations, and fears that are part and parcel of his daily work life. This is part of men's protective nature. After all, stress is supposed to be "no big deal" for them; to a degree, they are even expected to thrive on it. It would represent a loss of face for many men to admit that work affects them emotionally in such ways. "Nothing happened today" then becomes a very understandable, even normal response. Of course it has its downside, including the fact that it leads to isolation and presents a more or less constant temptation for men to comfort themselves, for example through drinking, or to distract themselves through some activity.

The man in this hypothetical example is not only protecting his partner and his self-image, but missing an opportunity for intimacy and connectedness. He is avoiding the opportunity for intimacy by minimizing his feelings. At most he might acknowledge that his interactions at work that day were annoying, implying again that there is no big deal here—nothing he cannot handle, or needs to communicate about or seek comfort for. Later on I will take a much closer look at the ways in which men resist intimacy. For now it is important to understand how this resistance relates to men's sense of themselves as men, and to their habit of not sharing their feelings.

Resisting the sort of intimate communication that women typically desire is actually a natural part of most men's defense of their identities. By the time they are married, most men have fifteen or twenty years of practice in doing this. Their habit does not in my opinion reflect some deep-seated resentment of their mothers (or by extension of women in general) in retaliation for feeling "controlled" by them as children. The explanation is simpler than that: this is the way men in our society believe they are supposed to be. To be otherwise would make them decidedly uncomfortable, perhaps even shameful. Their identity and self-esteem is based in part on being a stress absorber and a stoic. Ask them to start being intimate in the way that women want to be intimate, and they start feeling less manly.

This facet of being a man and its effects on men is supported by some hard data. For example, research on post-traumatic stress disorder (PTSD) reveals that although men as a group appear to be exposed to more traumatic stress than women are, they are less apt to report symptoms associated with PTSD.[82] On the other hand, men are much more likely to abuse alcohol and drugs than women are.[83] Both tendencies, of course, are connected. Men do not report fewer symptoms of PTSD because they are inherently more resilient than women are. Rather, their stoicism is just part of their expectations for themselves, and it contributes in turn to their greater vulnerability to substance abuse. It also contributes to the cultural secrecy that surrounds the physical, sexual, and emotional abuse of boys. We think of boys as tough and therefore treat them roughly, choosing to ignore their sensitivities; meanwhile, they perpetuate the situation by regarding it as unmasculine to complain.

Although we like to think of the Victorian era as history, a lot of men continue to try to live up to expectations that they will be strong, resilient, and to a degree, protective and self-sacrificing. These attributes have been associated with the heroic aspects of being male[84] for a long time—so long, in fact, that they seem like a part of men's nature. Despite their longevity, however, they may owe their origins less to biology than to those forces of history that pressed men to view themselves as self-controlled, tough, competitive, and worldly (in contrast to women, who were thought to be emotional, sensitive, noncompetitive, and domestic). There is nothing genetic, so far as I can see, about these sex-role differences. There is nothing in nature to account for why men should be considered tough, and women squeamish, when one considers how many men react to the idea of doing things like cleaning toilets or changing diapers.

The reason why many men report, day after day, that "nothing" happened at work that day is simply that they have an ingrained habit of not focusing on unpleasant feelings, along with a equally ingrained habit of protecting those who are close to them from unpleasant things. This protectionism and the tendency to absorb stress are dysfunctional in view of what women today want from men, but it nevertheless has a long tradition behind it, and it is an ethos that men still live by. In truth, life for most men—except, perhaps, for those few who have totally repressed them—is as replete with feelings as it is for women. But for a man, devoting too much time and attention to these aspects of his disenfranchised self represents a useless distraction at best and a dangerous threat to self-esteem at worst. So, unless he got fired, the company he works for went bankrupt, or his boss went crazy and shot twelve employees, nothing much happened at work.

For most women, events do not need to be especially dramatic to merit discussion. As opposed to protecting their partners from such stresses, they feel that it is decidedly desirable to talk about them. Therein lies the crux of the problem of intimacy that has become the most common complaint of women, and that is now also beginning to trouble men who want to find a better alternative to life than being a stress absorber, an addict, or both.

For example, Jay, a professional, has been dating Stacey for several months. He likes her very much, though at times he worries that she is too "aggressive." In particular, it makes him nervous when she questions him about what he is feeling if she thinks something may be bothering him, and when she confronts him with something that is bothering her. What disturbs him about these interactions is the "pressure," as he describes it, that she puts on him to respond to her. He confides in me that she "plays word games" with him, which he finds both confusing and frustrating. When I ask him what he means by word games, he replies, "She keeps at me, asking the same thing in twenty different ways. I don't know how to respond. It makes me want to run away. If she pressures me enough, I get angry, and later on I feel like a fool."

When it is her turn, Stacey describes Jay as a "nice man" who leads a stable life, is financially secure, and can be very sweet. She is not happy, however, about a pattern that has already developed where she is always the one to initiate affection and sex between them. Jay responds to her, she says, but it bothers her at times that he is so passive about it. It makes her uneasy when she thinks about her own parents' marriage, which was characterized by separate bedrooms and a decided lack of affection. She herself had never been very successful at getting her father's attention or affection. As a teen, she had a terrible self-image, tended to put on weight, dressed carelessly, and avoided dating. Now she is fairly slender, well dressed, and outgoing. She has a tendency to obsess about relationships, worrying more or less constantly if they are going well. She is doing that now with Jay.

During a joint counseling session, Stacey brings up the issue of sex. She shares her feelings of anxiety about Jay's passivity, saying it raises doubts in her mind about her attractiveness. On hearing this, Jay becomes obviously uncomfortable. Rather than truly listening to Stacey and trying to identify with her experience, he gets defensive. She is an attractive woman, he declares, and he cannot understand why she does not seem to see that. Turning to me, he complains that he cannot understand Stacey's insecurity about her looks. From his point of view she needs constant reassurance that she is attractive, and he finds that burdensome.

Stacey responds with anger. "That's what every man seems to say to me," she says. "They all seem to think I need too much."

"Maybe they've got a point," Jay shoots back sarcastically.

"Well, then," says Stacey, "maybe we should just go our separate ways."

Jay does not back off. "Maybe we should," he says. "Maybe you'll find that Mr. Right who won't let you down. I think I have a lot to offer in a relationship, and maybe I should be looking elsewhere, too."

At this point I interrupt. "I'm glad to hear that you feel you have a lot to offer in a relationship, Jay," I say. "I think it would be helpful, to you as much as to Stacey, if you could share your thoughts about that. What do you think you have to offer?"

Jay falls silent. I have just put him in the same situation he just complained about with Stacey, and I have done it on purpose. Not because I harbor any particular animosity for Jay; on the contrary, as a man I can identify with his discomfort. To go along with his implied threat, however, is not really doing him any favor. This is a strategy we men use all too often. It may succeed in arousing fears of rejection in whoever we are confronting, but it does nothing to build the relationship.

I press Jay to respond. I say I really want to know what he believes he has to offer.

"Well," Jay replies eventually. "I've worked very hard to get where I am. I'm a professional, and a reasonably successful one at that. I'm honest, and I'm loyal. I would think that there are many women out there who would value those things."

In offering this response, Jay is repeating a pattern I have come to know all too well. I and most of the men I have worked with have done it. Like Jay, we fall back on an old tradition, presenting what I would call our *positional credentials* to women and expecting them to love us. We believe that money and status are the things we bring into a relationship, and that if we do that we should somehow be excused from women's demands for intimacy or mutuality. More and more we find ourselves disappointed by the response we get, which is more and more likely to be the response that Jay got from Stacey.

Status and income can be important, just as loyalty and honesty are indeed valuable character traits. These things that men believe they have to offer, however, are best thought of as the basis for an alliance of sorts. We men have a right to value this kind of contribution to our relationships, but it is a mistake to delude ourselves that this is all it takes to make a relationship work today, or to satisfy the expectations of many women. If you doubt that, imagine what your response would be if the situation were reversed: if a woman told you that she was offering you a good income and loyalty, and she expected that that would be all you should be looking for in a relationship. How would that make you feel? Would it really be enough?

What men like Jay need to do is to focus less on their positional credentials and begin paying some attention to what *relational* credentials they have to offer. By this I mean things like the willingness to be intimate, including breaking old habits (such as stonewalling our partners when they express an interest in what happened to us that day) and learning new ones (such as learning to listen and identify). In addition, we need to develop a vocabulary of emotions and confront our fears of intimacy and mutuality. That is what this final part of the book is about.

Men's outlook on the world influences the way they connect with one another and their sense of what they mean by intimacy. Whereas women seem to establish relationships and experience intimacy largely through perceptions of shared responsibility, mutuality, and identification across a wide range of emotional experience, men do this primarily through the concept of alliance or teamwork, using a much narrower ranges of experience. While women connect with one another by talking about the things that concern them as much as the things that excite them, men's range of emotional communication with one another is decidedly limited because of their disenfranchised selves. Any emotion that is unmanly—and there are quite a few of them—is more or less outside the range of communication. The end result is simple: women are able to establish a much broader base of intimacy, and a sense of connection, than men are. Intimacy is, indeed, a common experience for women; this is not so for men.

When we speak of intimacy, the differences between what men and women mean are profound. For men, bondedness is based on the experience of alliance and loyalty, and intimacy is limited to identifying with one another mainly around common experiences in the competitive arena. Men can communicate and identify with one another (and feel intimate) around experiences associated with those feelings that relate to their shared concept of masculinity. The bonds that men can create in this way can be very strong; they are the strongest when the intimacy is based on a common ordeal. In his book *The Snow Leopard,* Peter Matthiessen recounts the personal ordeal he shared with the naturalist George Schaller as they trekked together across the Himalayas in search of the elusive leopard. Here is an example of the kind of intimacy that developed between these two men.

> High above the lake, GS turns to wait; he points at something on the trail. Coming up, I stare at the droppings and mute prints for a long time. All around are rocky ledges, a thin cover of stunted juniper and rose. "It might be close by, watching us," murmurs GS, "and we'd never see it." He collects the leopard scat, and we go on. On the mountain corner, in hard gusts of wind, GS's altimeter reads 13,300 feet.[85]
>
> By firelight, we talk about the snow leopard. Not only is it rare, so says GS, but it is wary and elusive to a magical degree, and so well camouflaged in the places it chooses to lie that one can stare straight at it from yards away and fail to see it. Even those who know the

mountains rarely take it by surprise; most sightings have been made by hunters lying still near a wild herd when a snow leopard happened to be stalking.[86]

One could argue, I suppose, that the snow leopard in this tale is a metaphor for male intimacy itself. It is in many instances an elusive and rare phenomenon, one that often catches us by surprise. Male intimacy is rooted in the idea of alliance, of being part of a team and depending on one another. Men bond together best, and intimacy most often emerges in the context of a competitive struggle against a common enemy (including, as in Matthiessen's book, nature). If the circumstances are right, however, men can also connect and feel intimate through working together, as the following example shows.

Mike decided to seek individual therapy in part because his relationship with his wife, Sarah, had been strained for so long that it verged on total alienation. It was also partly, to use his own words, because he was confused about his identity as a man. Sarah, he said, accused him of being incapable of intimacy; as we talked more, it became clear that it was communicative intimacy around a broad range of emotional experiences (basically, *female* intimacy) to which she was referring. And it was true that Mike, though from my perspective an emotional person, was hard-pressed to label his feelings (especially what he called the "sensitive" ones) and very reluctant to share them.

Mike was not at all unusual in feeling uncomfortable talking in depth about those thoughts and feelings that were foreign to his concept of himself as a man. He saw his role in life in large measure as a provider. He was a very loyal man, and even when things at work made him anxious he was inclined to "protect" (his word again) his family from these worries. Unfortunately, sharing these worries was precisely what Sarah, like most women, wanted to do. Moreover, she equated this, and this alone, with intimacy.

I asked Mike to think for a moment about times in his life when he felt most connected to someone else. At first, he shrugged. I persisted, asking him to relax for a moment and open his mind to memories associated with feeling really close to someone else. His gaze turned inward, and he fell silent. I waited; one gets used to this when talking with men about intimacy. Then, with a start, Mike looked up. "My God!" he said, more to himself than to me. I asked him to tell me what he was thinking about.

Mike told me he was raised in coastal Maine. He was the only child of a lobstering family that stretched back three generations. By virtue of his lack of brothers, he had been more or less obligated to learn the trade in order to help his father. Of his relationship with his mother he remembered very little—remarkably little, in fact. Eventually I came to believe that this was accounted for by the fact Mike had never bonded significantly with her. She had been a very aloof individual, someone who would put the food on the table every night but who never spoke much to him or touched him.

Mike's father worked a great deal. Not only did he run his lobster boat, but he had a side business, a small machine shop where he turned out odd jobs and made a highly variable income. According to Mike, his father would have given up lobstering in a minute had it not been for the fact that he just could not make enough money from his machining operation. Since he needed to lobster, and since hired help tended to eat up the profits, he took Mike along as often as he could from the time the boy was eight or nine.

Mike also disliked lobstering, which was little wonder given not only the hard nature of the work but the fact that he had been drafted into it. As an adolescent, he sometimes had to make the lobster runs alone if his father was ill or doing a rush job in the machine shop. Most of the time, though, the two did the rounds together. Mike explained what it was like to do this, and I must admit that it gave me pause; I had never realized just how dangerous lobstering could be. On clear, calm days it was hard work making the rounds of better than a hundred traps, but mostly it was boring.

In rough weather or fog, both of which are common along the Maine coast, lobstering is another matter entirely. Rocky shoals often lurk just beyond the limits of vision. Sometimes the sound of crashing waves can be a better indicator of potential trouble than anything in the line of sight. Squalls can appear out of nowhere and churn up ten-foot swells, and the tides can be treacherous. Out there Mike had learned the delicate art of driving a boat toward a shoal, riding the crest of a swell. As his father snagged a buoy, he would swing the bow around, then power swiftly away before the falling crest could bring the propeller down, perhaps upon a rock. On such days it could take two or three times as long to make the rounds, with father and son just barely beating the fast-sinking sun to shore.

When he went to college, Mike left lobstering behind forever. Successful as an executive, he nonetheless never again experienced anything like the excitement of those times on the water. His memory of intimacy, as jogged by our talk, was connected to it.

> My father and I rarely talked. Even when we did the run together, we could do the whole thing, which could take anywhere from two or three to six or seven hours, and not say more than twenty words the whole time. If there were more words than that, you could be sure they were all about the boat, the water, or the traps.
>
> But sometimes, especially on a sunny summer day when the water was calm and the air was almost warm—as warm as it gets on the water in Maine—my father would strip to the waist, go below, and come out with this old battery radio he kept in a watertight bag. He'd set it up by the wheel and turn it on loud and tune it in to some oldies station. Then he'd start to sing.
>
> He'd sing while he swung the boat from buoy to buoy and I hauled the traps. He sang so loud I swear you could have heard him ashore! After a while I'd join in, too. First I'd just hum along with him, but then I'd really sing. Pretty soon we'd be doing those old rock-and-roll songs in two-part harmony, as loud as we could sing. We'd do that for an hour or more. I can still remember it. I felt so close to him at those times. Is that what you mean by intimacy?

Mike's experience is a good example of male intimacy. It is a feeling of connection that comes through identification and a shared emotional experience—just like women's intimacy. But the circumstances that evoke it, and the range of feelings that form the basis for intimacy, are different for men.

The idea that men can not experience intimacy through verbal communication is nonsense. Men can and do talk, and they use talk to make connections with one another. What women may have a hard time understanding, however, is that the range of emotional experience that men feel open to communicating about is more limited, and that the kind of intimacy women are used to is therefore apt to be more an exception than the rule in men's relationships. Also, we need to appreciate how intimacy is connected with alliance in the minds of most men. This is true not only of so-called macho men, who after all represent only exaggerations of the male ideal, but also of men who would be shocked to be called macho but nevertheless buy into the masculine identity that includes toughness, resilience, competitiveness, and self-control as its cardinal virtues. They may balk just as much as the most macho street tough at the idea of being intimate in the same way that women are.

What exactly do women mean when they use the word *intimacy,* and how do they experience it? To illustrate this I will draw on material written by a woman. The following mother-daughter interaction is taken from the book *Refuge* by Terry Tempest Williams.

> Mother came over this morning.
> "Do you have a minute?" she asked. "Tamra Crocker Pulsifer was operated on yesterday for a brain tumor and I want to send her this letter. May I read it to you? I want it to be right."
> We walked into the living room. I opened the drapes and we settled on the couch. Mother paused, then began. . . .
> Dear Tammy:
> When I heard of your surgery yesterday, I felt my heart would break. I kept thinking that you are so young to have to go through this. I would gladly, Tammy, take this cross you are to bear upon my own shoulders if I could. I know what you are going through right now and I want you to know my prayers and love are with you.[87]

I dare say that most readers would agree that fathers and sons rarely have such interactions. A little later on in the book, Tammy replies as follows:

> Dear Diane:
> I feel you understand maybe far more than I do about this difficult time. The letter you sent was so good for me, and your constant support of myself and my mother have been deeply needed.[88]

This interchange strikes me as a good example of female intimacy. Like male intimacy, it is based on the notion of identification: the perception and appreciation of shared emotional experience. It is one person communicating that she understands and relates to what the other is going through. The content of the communication, however, is very different. Women openly share feelings of sadness and vulnerability much more readily than men do. Their form of intimacy therefore not only creates a bond, as men's does, but goes beyond that and becomes a powerful source of comfort. Through intimacy, women are able to transcend loneliness and unburden themselves of feelings like anxiety, grief, shame, and disappointment. Men do not do this because to do so would violate their sense of themselves as men. Virtually all of those emotions that make up the heart of female intimacy seem to be part of the disenfranchised selves of many men.

So how does a man react when a woman invites (or challenges) him to experience intimacy with her on *her* terms? Sadly, many men experience a woman's desire to communicate in the same way that she would with other women as something threatening and terrifying. It actually threatens the self-esteem of many men to be challenged to be intimate in this way. This is a testimonial to our disenfranchised selves, and also to our isolation.

In order to expand the boundaries of male intimacy, we men need to confront this idea that there are parts of ourselves that are in fact unacceptable to us and others, and to begin sharing them. We must find the courage to challenge our own anxiety and whatever shame we may feel when we begin to identify with each other's "unmanly" emotions and experiences.

12

How Men Resist Intimacy

Jack and Maggie had already separated once, for basically the same reasons that they were on the brink of separating again. Jack, a recovering alcoholic and active AA member with more than fifteen years of sobriety, had rebuilt his life out of the ashes that booze had made of it. Though obviously weathered by his years of drinking, Jack was still a handsome man, with an athletic build that even a mild case of overeating and a lack of exercise could not entirely hide. He was in many ways what they call a man's man: always up for a fishing trip, a ballgame, or (in the old days) a night of drinking and carousing. He enjoyed competition and, until he was derailed by drinking, had been on the corporate fast track. Now he worked as a substance abuse counselor in a small private residential setting. He liked what he did but was also aware that he might eventually get bored with it, and so he was contemplating returning to graduate school to earn a degree that would expand his horizons as a therapist.

Jack met Maggie, who was also a recovering alcoholic, when they both had been sober for about three years. Their shared commitment to recovery, and to the ideas and values expressed in the twelve steps and traditions, formed the backdrop for their romance and eventual commitment to each other. Though that commitment was still evident, their marriage itself was slowly dying of neglect. To some degree they both were responsible, though clearly Jack was the one who was most responsible for failing to nurture his marriage in the same way that he nurtured his sobriety, and for resisting being intimate in the way that Maggie needed him to be.

Jack spent several hours a week at meetings, plus a couple of hours on the phone with AA friends, his own sponsor, and two people he sponsored. He clearly saw the need to do this in the interest of his recovery. Nevertheless, he resisted Maggie's continued efforts to get him to spend time with her or to communicate with her. He much preferred to watch sports on television (in the cold months) or go fishing (in the spring, summer, and fall). If she asked him to talk with her, the conversation invariably turned to fishing or sports. He said he hated talking about work (though I later learned that he would do that in order to avoid having to talk about his feelings).

After a while Maggie sought refuge in her own work as a way of distracting herself from her dissatisfaction and loneliness. When I first met her, she was working two jobs for a total of nearly sixty hours a week. The issue of intimacy in her marriage to Jack was obvious, it seemed, to everyone except him. He was blind to the obvious: that his marriage was slipping away while he watched basketball and fished.

Things went on in this frustrating way through more than a year of marriage counseling. Confrontation after confrontation could not get Jack to budge in terms of his willingness to devote more time to interacting with Maggie, to talk about what went on in his life at work eight hours a day, or to discuss what he felt in his heart. He only complained that he worked too much for too little money. If Maggie pressed him, he would get irritable and snap at her, usually succeeding in putting her on the defensive.

I sensed a crisis in the making when it came to light in one of our sessions that Maggie had taken to spending time with a man she had met at a coffee shop. He was a regular, as was she, though for different reasons. She came there twice a week after an early morning AA meeting; he was a local merchant, divorced, who ate breakfast and read the morning paper there as a daily ritual. Their relationship started very casually and had progressed slowly. Maggie liked him for the simple reason that he was actually interested in what she had to say—in other words, because they *talked*. Sometimes they would sit together, but more often they would talk to each other from adjoining tables. This, I learned, had been going on for about six months. It came to light only because Jack had wandered into the restaurant one morning and spotted the two of them talking and laughing. He brought it up in our session, but Maggie just brushed it off.

A couple of months later, Jack came to our session upset. This time he had come home from work early one day and found Maggie and her "friend" sitting on their back porch, drinking coffee and talking. He demanded to know what was going on. Maggie turned on him angrily. "Nothing's going on!" she said. "This is just a friend. We *talk* together. Is that a crime? *You* don't want to talk to me!"

Sadly, Jack missed even this blatant warning. In front of him, I asked Maggie for the hundredth time what it was that she wanted from Jack. She replied for the hundredth time that she wanted some attention and communication. "I feel like I'm married to a wooden Indian!" she said.

Again, Jack did not hear it, or at least he heard it wrong. He heard Maggie demanding something from him, and his response was to dig his heels in. No matter how I tried to frame it, to help him see that it was intimacy Maggie was looking for, he kept hearing it as a demand and a threat. Finally, he said to Maggie, "Look, Maggie, this is me. Take it or leave it." Three months later, she left.

Problems of intimacy like the one that destroyed Jack's marriage are painfully common. The irony is that men continue to choose alienation and loneliness—and to persist in their commitment to a model of masculinity that is outdated, is relationally dysfunctional, and makes them vulnerable to addiction—when expanding their capacity for intimacy is what they need and is often there for the taking. The truth is that Jack actively *resisted* intimacy; the story of lost intimacy and love, of relationships that fail, is often no more complicated or hard to understand than that. Then again, the story of addiction and its losses is often surprisingly simple to understand. The answer to why men often do nothing while their relationships turn to ashes may be very close to the answer to another question: how can men stand by and watch their lives turn into ashes while they pursue alcohol, drugs, work, sex, or gambling compulsively? They do both in large part because they develop strong habits of avoiding emotions.

Recovery from addiction has parallels in the relational realm. People in recovery from addiction, as well as those millions who have turned to twelve-step fellowships for other reasons, are familiar with the word *denial*. They use it to refer to the ways in which individuals resist facing up to reality. In the case of addiction, it is the reality of powerlessness over the compulsion to drink, use drugs, gamble, and so on, plus the unmanageability that addiction creates in his life, that the addict refuses to face.

The concept of denial and the idea of resisting reality can also be applied to relationships. With respect to intimacy, what we can deny or avoid includes the reality that we have all had the same feelings at one time or another, that we can identify with each other's emotional experiences, and that doing so makes us feel connected to one another. We can also resist accepting the fact that a chronic lack of intimacy is an aversive state that has definite effects on our well-being and on our ability to grow as individuals.

In order to be intimate, we need to be able to do two things: to reveal our true feelings, and to identify with the emotional experience of the other person. In other words, intimacy requires being open and also being receptive. We can block intimacy either by holding back, or by refusing to identify. As discussed in the last chapter, and contrary to popular belief, men can be intimate; however, the range and depth of emotional intimacy experienced by women is typically much greater than that experienced by men. The disenfranchised self that leads men to edit their emotional experience and their willingness to share it largely accounts for this.

Hidden somewhat between the lines in the quotation from Harry Stack Sullivan at the beginning of this part of the book is the realization that we need relationships in order to grow. I believe this is true. Those men I know who have resisted intimacy the longest and the hardest are the sickest—spiritually and psychologically speaking—men I know. They are also the most immature.

Relationships need intimacy if they are to thrive. As we all know, the initial attraction that draws two people together can sustain a relationship early on. If intimacy fails to develop, however, that relationship will eventually either break up or slowly decline into a state of mutual alienation. If you think of intimacy as the we-factor—meaning that in a relationship there is *you, me* and *we*—then intimacy is what keeps the we-factor alive and enables it to grow. Relationships, like individuals, either grow and mature or else remain immature. Intimacy is what makes the difference between a growing relationship and a stagnant one. By extension, vital relationships are what enables individuals to grow.

Before we can begin looking at how to be intimate, we need to understand how this concept of denial applies to relationships. Men need to understand *how* they resist intimacy in their relationships; in other words, they need to understand the forms that this resistance takes within themselves. In my experience, men can become very conscious of this once they understand it and pay attention to it.

I believe it is equally important for us to understand how men resist intimacy as it is to understand why they do it. Becoming intimate in many respects is not so much a matter of *doing* something as it is of letting go of resistance to doing it. As we look at some of the more common ways that men resist intimacy, it is likely that you will be able to identify with several of them. Certainly Jack in the above example used virtually all of these methods in order to avoid being intimate with Maggie, and he was not unusual.

It can be helpful in trying to increase your capacity for intimacy to be able to put labels on the various ways a person can resist it. The labels I use for the most common forms of resisting intimacy are stonewalling, minimizing/maximizing, rationalizing, distracting, attacking, pseudochoice, and dissuasion. Each of these is discussed below.

The first and simplest form that resistance to intimacy takes is what I call *stonewalling*. With respect to addiction the term means refusing to talk about the problem, as if that would make it go away. The stonewalling alcoholic, for example, simply refuses to talk about his drinking. Whenever someone brings up the issue, he proclaims that they are making a big deal about nothing, are out to get him, or are just plain wrong. No matter how obvious it is to an outsider that the addict's life may be falling apart, he stubbornly refuses to discuss it. If that does not work, then he may just get up and walk out.

Does this sound familiar? Does stonewalling operate in relationships? Of course it does. Jack, our case in point, first tried to stonewall by trying to convince Maggie that everything was really fine and that she was making a "big deal over nothing." When this stopped working he took another tack, claiming that pressures at work were making it difficult for him to commit to weekly appointments. Finally, at the point in our work when things were at their worst—when he and Maggie were at their most alienated, and she was starting to build another relationship—Jack asked me if I thought that a "break" from therapy would help! When I suggested that this sounded like pure avoidance, he got angry; maybe what their marriage needed, he persisted, was *less* talk. Maggie looked at him in disbelief. I tried to talk with him about this, but his ears were closed. He dropped out of therapy for a month after that.

Stonewalling happens all the time in relationships, and men use it more than women, I think, as a defense. It is a way we have of maintaining our image of ourselves as strong and invulnerable, even when that image results in our own alienation and destroys our relationships.

Another common form of resistance is *minimizing/maximizing*. This is a two-sided process in which the individual simultaneously minimizes his own problems and exaggerates (maximizes) those of others. The effect is to draw a false contrast that makes it seem as though the individual's problems are relatively minor. In the area of addiction, a cocaine abuser might downplay his own use ("I only use on weekends, and I'm doing fine at work") while exaggerating the use and problems of others ("I have a friend who's into crack and just got fired for embezzling"). The implication, of course, is that this person really has no problem when compared with others.

Minimizing/maximizing in relationships can take on two different forms, the simplest of which pretty much straightforwardly models what happens in addiction. Jack tried to contrast his marriage to Maggie with those of others they knew whom he thought were worse off. He talked about couples he knew who fought all the time, and couples where one partner was still actively drinking or using. The intended effect, of course, was to avoid having to deal with the issue of intimacy between him and Maggie by attempting to make their relationship seem relatively better.

Intimacy is created by openness and by identification with the experience (especially the emotional experience) of another person. Another way to put it is that two people feel intimate when they are able to share and validate each other's emotional experiences. Some men resist intimacy by denying (minimizing) the similarities between their partner's experience and their own. At the same time, they often exaggerate (maximize) the differences between their own experience and that of their partner. One example of this is the man who doggedly insists, "We have absolutely nothing in common." Another is the man who consistently refuses to validate the experience of his partner ("I can't understand why you feel that way. I feel completely different").

Of course, there are times when we may honestly have a hard time relating to exactly how someone else thinks or feels. But when this is a persistent pattern in situations that most people could identify with, then it is most likely resistance to intimacy that's responsible. Few couples really have absolutely nothing in common. More likely, the truth is that one partner does not want to have anything in common with the other.

The third form of resistance to intimacy is *rationalizing*. The classic example of rationalizing, taken from the alcoholism field, goes like this: "If you were married to my wife, you'd drink, too." You can replace the word *wife* in this sentence with any other one you like. Aside from wives (or husbands), jobs, children, physical problems, dysfunctional families, and unhappy childhoods are often used as rationalizations for drinking or drug abuse. Sometimes an effort to evoke sympathy, and perhaps even a little guilt, is added in for good measure: "If you only knew how unhappy I am," the addict laments, or "If you'd gone through what I've gone through," or "If you were only more understanding . . . "

Work is a favorite excuse men use to rationalize their avoidance of intimacy. "I have too much work to do," they say, implying that they are much too busy to waste time on something unimportant, like relating. They may also throw in a dose of guilt: "Your demands [for intimacy] are interfering with my work."

Rationalizing can be convincing at times, but when you look below the surface it becomes transparent. The idea that personal interests or ambitions leave no room for intimacy is absurd, especially if you believe (as I do) that intimacy is a fundamental human psychological need and that it is absolutely vital to personal growth. If you try to do without intimacy, you are fated to a life of isolation and immaturity and are highly vulnerable to turning to one form of addiction or another as a compensation.

There are no viable excuses for not being intimate. Intimacy is created whenever two people identify with each other on a feeling level; in other words, when they can validate and relate to each other's emotional experience. Emotions are the currency of intimacy, and here men and women share a common core. Excitement is excitement, frustration is frustration, joy is joy, grief is grief, and so on. Regardless of the particulars of experience, we all share a great deal of common ground, emotionally speaking. Therefore, we share the basis for intimacy. The difference between men who are intimate and those who are not has a lot to do with how willing they are to venture into their disenfranchised selves and open them up to the light of day.

Distraction is another tool that we can use in the interests of avoiding intimacy. Talk to an active alcoholic about drinking, and what happens? Before long, and usually without you realizing it, you are talking about something else. Typically it is another problem, often one that is tempting to talk about. That is distraction at work. The cleverer the addict, the better he is at distracting communication away from his addiction. In relationships, men can be very adept at getting off the topic of their own or their partner's feelings.

Despite the fact that we were ostensibly meeting to talk about their marriage and about Maggie's feelings of "intimacy starvation," as she once put it, Jack would often attempt to control the agenda of our sessions and get us away from that topic. He would often jump in at the start of sessions with his pet distraction, which was his job—how poorly he was paid, and the long hours he put in. When I pointed out this pattern, Maggie said that the same thing happened whenever she tried to talk to Jack about their relationship. "He always changes the subject," she complained. She admitted that it made her angry, but it also made her feel guilty: "I feel like I should be interested. But what I really feel is resentment that we always end up talking about his job."

Distraction that is cleverly done often puts us in the kind of bind that Maggie described. I supported Maggie's desire to talk about her and Jack's relationship. I said that talking about feelings was "the most important thing in a relationship, more important even than talking about work." Again, Jack looked annoyed.

Many spouses have had the uncomfortable experience of trying to confront an addict about his or her drug use, only to find themselves on the defensive about how much *they* drank as a college student, or about some problem they have with money, sex, or anything else that gets off the issue. These are examples of *attack*, which is really just another form of distraction. In relationships, attacking allows us to get angry and thereby avoid having to be open about our other feelings, or having to identify with the other person's feelings. Anger usually makes the other person feel scared, guilty, or angry in return. In the process, an opportunity for intimacy gets lost.

For example, Alice, Bob's partner, experienced all of these reactions at times when Bob would fly off the handle and storm out of the house. He would do this whenever she tried to confront him about something and to share with him how she felt about it, or when she pushed him to express his feelings about something. Bob had been abused and neglected as a child, and his way of avoiding intimacy was an aggressive one. He acknowledged that it made him very edgy to have to talk about how he felt, or to have to listen to how Alice felt. He thought of himself as an unemotional person—a sure sign of resistance to intimacy and of a rigidly disenfranchised self. He short-circuited communication, and thereby intimacy, by getting instantly defensive and then attacking.

Yet another form of resistance that is important to understand is something I call *pseudochoice*. Like all the forms of resistance I am discussing here it serves a single purpose, which is to avoid having to reveal ourselves or identify with the other person. This particular way of avoiding relies on simple bluff: the individual (assumed here to be male for discussion purposes) claims that he *wants* things to be the way they are. In other words, he asserts that he is *choosing* to be the way he is, meaning in this case someone who chooses not to be intimate. The alcoholic whose drinking-related problems finally catch up to him may turn around and say, in effect, "I know that drinking gets me into trouble, but I'm not really addicted—drinking is just what I want to do."

As transparent as it is, pseudochoice makes its appearance regularly in couples counseling as a means of resisting intimacy. Men can be as obviously in need of intimacy as any desperate alcoholic is of sobriety, yet insist that they do not need or want it. They try to convince others that they really do not *want* to feel close, or to communicate. They imply that they prefer to live a life of emotional isolation and may even go so far as to try to claim that this is healthy, and that others' desire for intimacy is somehow abnormal.

The last form of resistance to intimacy that I help men look for in themselves is *dissuasion*. Especially in the hands of a clever man, dissuasion can be an especially subtle and effective defense. Like all of the other defenses discussed here, it serves to prevent us from identifying with the other person's emotional reality and thereby feeling connected to them. In this case, we do this by denying *their* emotional reality; in effect, we try to talk them out of their feelings. They say they are sad and we deny it, for example, by trying to convince them that they should not be. Some men may combine dissuasion with distraction by telling someone they should not be sad and then talking about something else or making a joke. If we are really clever the other person may actually end up feeling better, at least temporarily, even though we have cheated them out of their feelings. We may extend this tactic and try to dissuade someone from what they think, or even what they see or hear. Eventually, dissuasion leads to resentment or depression in the other person.

Another patient, Fritz, was a master of dissuasion. A therapist, he had a better facility with psychological jargon than anyone I had ever met. He was financially successful, outspoken, and intellectually intimidating. A good many people, I knew, also thought him arrogant and self-centered. His wife, Martha, was much quieter and plainspoken than he was. She was also, I thought, rather depressed, and as I watched them interact I saw why. Whenever Martha tried to talk honestly with Fritz about how she felt, he would immediately go to work dissuading her from her feelings. He would directly challenge her most obvious feeling statements. "I don't think you're really angry, Martha," he'd say, "I think you're jealous," or "You tell me you're sad and upset with me, but I suspect it's guilt that you're really feeling," and so on. No wonder Martha was depressed: no matter what she said, Fritz made it into something else. She had been telling him for years that she did not feel that there was any real intimacy or connectedness between them. He tried to dissuade her from that feeling, too, arguing that it was depression that was her problem, not a lack of intimacy.

I suggest that male readers take some time now to do some more journal writing. Do a personal inventory of the ways in which you have resisted intimacy in your relationships in the past, and how you might do this now. This may not be an easy task. It can take courage, not to mention a good deal of reflection, to be this honest with yourself.

In taking a personal inventory of this sort, begin by trying to identify with *all* of the above forms of denial. Each of us has probably used every one of them at some point. Identify several specific examples of how you may have used each of the above methods to resist intimacy in a relationship at least once. Then identify your two or three most frequently used forms of resistance.

Once you have completed this personal inventory, and if you have been working together with other men in a growth group, consider sharing your thoughts about this issue of resisting intimacy with each other. Take turns doing this. As you listen to each other, try to identify with each other's experiences of avoiding intimacy.

Part of your work from now on will be to become more aware of times when you avoid opportunities for intimacy. The key will lie in your discomfort when someone else begins to express a feeling, or when they ask you to share your own feelings. The discomfort will most likely be connected to your disenfranchised self: that part of you that you associate with being unmanly. It will tempt you to use one form of resistance or another in order to avoid the situation. In doing so you will have defended your image of yourself, but you will very likely also have missed a chance to build more of a connection between yourself and the person with whom you are in a relationship.

13

Becoming Intimate

Intimacy demands two things: identification and emotional openness. It is that simple. The problem for men is that the range of their own emotional experience that is acceptable to them, that they can accept in others, and about which they are able to be open is limited. As a rule, men will react with discomfort whenever someone else is revealing an emotion that is part of their own disenfranchised selves. For instance, if a man has disenfranchised sadness from his concept of himself, so that being a man is tied into not feeling sad, then he will get uncomfortable when someone else expresses sadness. Many men I know get edgy and even angry when a woman cries. Rather than identify with her sadness, they run from it, using one or another of the forms of resistance described in the last chapter. Similarly, many a man has disenfranchised dependency—the desire for support and comfort—from his self-concept. Any expression of emotion along those lines makes him very uncomfortable. Since he cannot accept the emotions associated with wanting support and comfort in himself, he rejects them in others as well. Again, instead of identifying, he runs the other way. The consequences are a lack of intimacy in the relationship and a sense of isolation in the man.

In order to expand the depth of intimacy that men are open to, what is needed is a reevaluation of our basic ideas about masculinity, a decision to be different, and the courage to experiment with being more balanced. To experience intimacy does not mean that men have to throw away their ability to experience bonding through alliance, that they need to reject every facet of traditional masculinity, or even that they have to give up competitiveness altogether. If what they want is to grow in relationships and reduce their vulnerability to addiction, however, then men do need to move toward a better balance between the positional and relational orientations. They need to learn to define themselves not just in terms of who they are with respect to their credentials and their place in society, but of who they are with respect to what they feel, and the important attachments they have nurtured.

For us men to change it can help to take a look at ourselves in perspective—to take stock of just how much we are driven by biology versus cultural tradition, and what choices we therefore have. In order to break free of the bonds created by a male role that has limited us at the same time that it has defined us, we need to open ourselves to discovering what intimacy can be and what it can do for us, just as we need to reevaluate self-esteem and how we can achieve it.

Perhaps the greatest relational challenge facing a man is to be able to see the world through a woman's eyes. Some who believe in profound and irreconcilable sex differences would say that this is simply impossible. Others argue that men and women are really not that much different from each other. I tend to believe in sex differences; to me, it is not unreasonable to expect that two sexes that are different anatomically and hormonally, and for whom at least some differences in behavior are evident across cultures,[89] would also be different to some extent both temperamentally and psychologically. In fact, it seems naive to think otherwise. But I also believe that these differences are not as exaggerated as Victorian stereotypes would suggest. Rather, they represent a challenge and an opportunity for growth. Intimacy is the vehicle for this growth.

Intimacy—being able to step into another person's shoes and identify with their experience—is an antidote to loneliness and anxiety. It is food for the hungry heart. I believe that we need intimacy psychologically in much the way that we need food on a physical level. But men have been so well socialized to fear and avoid intimacy, and are so unschooled in it, that they now need help understanding how to change their beliefs and approach it. In the last chapter I looked at how men avoid intimacy. Now I will take a look at some of the things that men can do to begin expanding their capacity for it.

"I've got my life organized into compartments," Brad said proudly. "I'm able to shift from one compartment to another whenever I need to. I can leave the others behind just like that." He snapped his fingers for emphasis. "That's how I can handle as many things as I do."

Brad was responding to my question about how he managed all of the responsibilities in his life. Aside from having a demanding full-time job as a building contractor, he was studying for a graduate degree in business, also on a full-time basis. Recently remarried, he lived with his new wife, Maria, and her six-year-old son. They had just bought an older house that needed quite a bit of work, much of which he was doing himself. His teenage daughter from his first marriage spent most weekends with him and Maria. The kids, especially his, had been giving the two of them a hard time, which was ostensibly why they had come to see me.

Though she was subtle about how she said it, I perceived that Maria was having a hard time dealing with the stress of trying to establish a new marriage, make a home, and negotiate the treacherous waters of stepparenthood while living with a man who was a compulsive worker. She looked a bit frayed around the edges. It did not help, I suspected, that Brad resisted identifying with how she felt.

Tall and solidly built, Brad could look very intimidating when he got angry. This happened whenever we touched on the issue of Maria's stress, or how she felt about having to manage all of the complex relationships in her life. Brad invariable tried to minimize or discount her feelings. Or he would draw the conversation to himself, complaining about how hard he had to work to support the family. If all else failed, he would try putting Maria on the defensive by accusing her of harboring a double standard for her child versus his.

Brad indeed worked hard, but it was obvious to me (as another man) that he did this for himself—in other words, in the interest of his positionally based self-esteem—even though he claimed to be doing it for Maria and the kids. And though he tried to convince us about how he was able to "compartmentalize" his life, I knew he was only fooling himself. He was trying to be strong and self-controlled, and to achieve that place in life that he associated with self-esteem, and I had little doubt that many of the emotions Maria was expressing (such as her stress and loneliness) were also part of his own disenfranchised self. The tension was obvious to anyone who looked at him; he was as wired as any man I had ever met. Having failed once in business, and still smarting from it, he was now driven to succeed. I suspected he harbored doubts about his ability to achieve the financial goals he so boldly boasted about, but he denied this when I brought it up. He never doubted for a second, he said, that he would be spectacularly successful.

In his relationship with Maria, Brad had no tolerance for conflict, little patience, and almost no willingness to compromise. If asked to give something up—from something as minor as a business dinner to something as major as an elective graduate course—in the interest of a better marriage or family life, he would all but fly into a rage. In no uncertain terms he would make clear that such a sacrifice was impossible. In large part I thought this reflected his inability to compromise with himself and rein in his obsession with success.

I also discovered that Brad had few friends, and none at all who were not related in some way through business. He socialized more or less exclusively with men who worked for him, or else men he worked for. According to Maria, he was keenly conscious of people's social status and often joked about some supposed friends being "losers." He was also a jealous and possessive man. In an argument with Maria, he would often bring up one of her past boyfriends and put him down while simultaneously challenging her, growling, "I suppose you would have been happier with [name], that loser!" He did this once in my office, and I remember thinking that there might come a day when he would get a shocking response from Maria.

On a day-to-day basis it took very little to push Brad over the edge. Just a slight change in plans could be enough to provoke an angry attack, and his being upset was always somehow Maria's fault. The theme, of course, was control. Brad, it seemed, wanted to control virtually everything from what Maria did with her time (almost literally from hour to hour) to who she socialized with to what, if anything, she did to earn money.

As difficult as I imagined it would be to live with Brad, in part I found myself feeling sympathy for him. He was so driven to succeed, and so preoccupied with control, that I felt certain it was only a matter of time before he got some sort of physical ailment, destroyed his marriage, or both. I took a chance and told him that he seemed committed to trying to pretend that he really was not stressed out, that he really had everything under control. He looked at me with a trace of anger in his eyes. "But I'm not trying to pretend anything," he said. "I really can have things under control, and I really could manage all the stress in my life—that is, if Maria would only cooperate!"

Brad was a very insecure and overcompensated man. He was intensely competitive and jealous. I learned that whenever he and Maria were in a mixed group, he spent much of his time sizing up the other men, comparing himself to them in terms of how attractive they were, how successful they were, and so on. He actually tortured himself by being obsessed over these things. Little wonder he had no real male friends, felt isolated, and (as he finally admitted) occasionally suffered from anxiety attacks.

Though he would never say so, Brad actually expected Maria to accept having to fit her life around his. He wanted her to clear all plans she might make, whether or not they involved him, in advance. He wanted her to talk to him before she made any new friends, since he might have reservations about them. He also expected her to run the household virtually single-handed. Fortunately (for I suspected that otherwise she would end up divorcing him), Maria would not go along. Her resistance, in turn, was what forced the issue of intimacy between them to the forefront. And intimacy *was* the issue just as much as control, since Brad staunchly resisted getting into Maria's shoes and really understanding what she was experiencing and feeling. That in large part was what enabled him to continue pressuring her as much as he did.

Brad's tactics for resisting intimacy ran the gamut. He would change the topic from his unrealistic expectations to her supposed "oppositionalism," and she would have to think about that. He would accuse her of playing favorites with the children, and again she would have to think and defend herself. He would complain that she was unsympathetic to how hard he worked, and she would feel guilty. He would also say that she had in effect broken her word to support his decision to go to graduate school, with the same effect. He would say that she was exaggerating their problems, and that they actually had a much better relationship and family life than most of their friends did. If all else failed, he would suggest that if she was so unhappy maybe she should move out. These tactics were employed whenever Maria would try to explain how she was feeling about her life and her relationship with Brad. Rather than identify with and approach her, he would get defensive in one or more of these ways and push her away. In each instance another opportunity for intimacy was lost. Brad's defensiveness and his work addiction was slowly but surely eroding his marriage. There was too much *me,* not enough *we.*

As the months went by and our work together dragged along, I could see more and more how Brad resisted connecting with Maria. I also sensed the alienation between them starting to set in. After six months, he started to complain that she was "turning cold" and rejecting his sexual advances. I offered the explanation that maybe Maria was not feeling intimate with Brad. While she nodded, he worked himself into a snit, accusing her of trying to control him through sex.

Knowing the kind of woman she was and the way she had dealt with feeling trapped and frustrated in her first marriage, I could not see Maria staying with Brad forever—in spite of how much she wanted this marriage to work—if he did not change. That change had to begin, I knew, with getting Brad to drop his resistances to intimacy. He needed to stop distracting, minimizing, rationalizing, and attacking, and to start identifying with Maria's emotional reality. He needed to be able to get into her shoes and validate her experience. This would put their relationship on an equal footing and set the stage for negotiation and compromise. It would create intimacy, but it would no doubt also make Brad feel vulnerable and anxious. Yet this was the only way, I believed, that his marriage could survive and grow in the long run.

Working with men as tough and determined as Brad is not easy. They are not receptive to being challenged, particularly about their basic personality and how it may be standing in the way of intimacy. As discussed in previous chapters, their self-esteem is based on personal attributes (like competitiveness and detachment) that are conducive to establishing and defending a niche in the world, but not to attachment and intimacy. Consequently, these men are afraid to let go of their defenses.

In Brad's case, the strategy I took involved politely interrupting him whenever he got going on a roll of distracting, minimizing, or attacking. I would say something like, "I hear what you're saying,

Brad, but let's both see if we can get into Maria's shoes for a moment and see how *she* feels." Then, after she spoke, I pressed him to share his perceptions of how she felt. At times I knew I was making him irritated; in truth, I was not always sure he would come back for more. But he did—because, I believe, he really loved Maria and wanted his marriage to work. Also, as he said to me reluctantly once when we met alone, he felt that some things I said about his feeling isolated and insecure struck a chord somewhere inside him.

Despite the difficulties of the work, it paid off. It took a while for Brad to feel safe doing what I was asking him to do. After a while, though, I would be able to ask him to stay in Maria's shoes for a while and explain what he would be thinking, feeling, and inclined to do next if he were her. As he did this, I could almost feel the bond between them growing.

In time Brad became better at not only identifying with Maria's feelings, but also identifying and communicating his own feelings at any given time. This process gradually moved their relationship to an entirely new plane, one that Brad admitted made him feel vulnerable at times. But he also said he could only envision himself going further down this road in the future.

The process of learning to drop defenses and gradually identify more and more with another person has profound effects on men and their relationships. It is a pathway to intimacy that most men are inclined to avoid for two reasons. First, it is a process that tends to erase any sense of difference that separates two people. If you want to feel different from—and especially if you want to feel better than—someone else, the last thing you want to do is to put yourself in their shoes and see the world through their eyes. Since men's orientation toward themselves and others is founded on competition and the perception of difference, identification on an emotional level can be psychologically threatening. Second, identifying with someone else's emotional experience naturally invites one to share in return. Many of the emotions that men want to avoid in others are the very same ones that they want to avoid in themselves. Another way to think of it is that intimacy threatens to expose the disenfranchised self. A man like Brad, as described above, feels uncomfortable and unmanly when he shares feelings that he has chronically suppressed because they are inconsistent with his image of himself.

Learning to stop resisting and to start identifying provides the one really effective way I have discovered so far for dealing with the eternal complaint that men are out of touch with their feelings. No matter how hard I have seen men try, they never seem to be able to get in touch with their feelings simply by trying harder. That approach is just another manifestation of the old archetype of masculinity at work: faced with frustration, a good man simply tries harder. This always seems to backfire when it comes to identifying emotions and becoming intimate. I can picture men now, sitting on therapists' couches across the country, struggling to "get in touch" with themselves through sheer white-knuckle determination!

Instead of fighting with themselves, the approach advocated here holds that men would do better to follow Brad's path, getting in touch with their feelings by dropping their defenses against intimacy and learning to identify with how someone else is feeling. The more insecure a man is, the more helpless he is apt to be in breaking through his own emotional block through force of will. The best, and perhaps only, way for him to do this may be the indirect route—to dismantle his wall of denial and discover what is on the other side.

The following exercise is one that a man can work on individually. Like most of the other work presented here, though, it is much more effective when it is done in the context of a men's growth group. Even though one of our aims is to be intimate with women, men need to learn to be intimate with one another as well. In many ways, it may be easier to open up and identify with our partners after we have faced our anxieties about opening up with each other.

Begin by identifying those emotions you feel most comfortable revealing. You can use the following list as a guide, but feel free to add others. Think of specific situations in which you have been able to express any or all of these emotions:

anger	sadness	excitement	sexual desire
frustration	grief	joy	fear
shame	guilt	happiness	boredom
loneliness	anxiety	love	affection

• Try to connect the expression of each emotion with a specific situation in which you expressed it. Which of the above emotions are the ones that you reveal least often?

- Is there any pattern in who you are able to express certain emotions with? For example, are you able to share feelings of sadness with particular people but not others? What feeling(s) can you share primarily or exclusively with women as opposed to men (and vice-versa)?
- Put together a list of those emotions that you have shared least often with other people. Now imagine a man who *did* express these feelings fairly often with others. What would you think of such a man? Would you want to be like him, or does that idea make you uncomfortable?
- To what extent do you think your list of "taboo" emotions belong to your disenfranchised self? How comfortable are you when someone else tries to express these feelings to you? Can you think of any specific instances in which you got uncomfortable (or even angry) when your partner tried to express one of these emotions?

Think of becoming intimate as a process of gradually revealing your disenfranchised self and being able to identify with the emotional experience (including emotions you are uncomfortable with) of someone else. A men's growth group may be as good a place as any to begin this process of unfolding. As indicated above, you may find it most productive to try to catch yourself resisting identification with one feeling or another that someone else is expressing. If that is the case, take a risk and share your perception of your own resistance. Tell the group about your discomfort with these emotions, and what you want to do when you hear someone express them.

Once you have been able to accept your resistance you may find, as many others have, that you are gradually able to step into the other person's shoes just long enough to identify with their feelings. Once there, you may still feel uncomfortable; if so, share it. The most likely reason for your discomfort is that what the other person is feeling is something that you do not like to accept in yourself. You will not grow very much, and your relationships will lack intimacy, so long as you choose to reject this part of your emotional self and reject it in others as well.

Growth groups that have been working together for a while, and that have already done some of the work on self-esteem described in the second part of this book, may be most ready to move toward exploring the potential of intimacy. As they do, they will discover that any feelings of isolation that have troubled them over the years will slowly begin to fade. Alienation and chronic frustration will start to give way to periods of serenity. Self-hatred will be replaced by self-acceptance. The reason will be that these men will be moving toward a more connected view of themselves in relation to others, and in the process will be discovering the power of intimacy both to heal and to nurture us.

Notes

1. *Alcoholics Anonymous*, 3rd ed. New York: Alcoholics Anonymous World Services, 1976.
2. R. Room. *Alcoholics Anonymous as a Social Movement*. Toronto, Ontario, Canada: Addiction Research Foundation, 1992.
3. Room, *Alcoholics Anonymous as a Social Movement*.
4. *Comments on A.A.'s Triennial Surveys*. New York: Alcoholics Anonymous General Services Office, 1990.
5. *Alcoholics Anonymous 1989 Membership Survey*. New York: Alcoholics Anonymous General Services Office, 1990.
6. National Institute on Drug Abuse and National Institute on Alcohol Abuse and Alcoholism. *Highlights from the 1987 National Drug and Alcoholism Treatment Unit Survey (NDATUS)*. Rockville, MD: NIDA/NIAAA, 1989.
7. J. Helzer and T. R. Pryzbeck. "The co-occurrence of alcoholism with other psychiatric disorders in the general population and its impact on treatment." *Journal of Studies on Alcoholism*, 49(3):219–224, 1988.
8. G. A. Marlatt and J. R. Gordon, eds. *Relapse Prevention: Maintenance Strategies in the Treatment of Addictive Behaviors*. New York: Guilford, 1985.
9. *Comments on A.A.'s Triennial Surveys*.
10. N. Chodorow. "Family structure and personality." In M. Z. Rosaldo and L. Lamphere, eds., *Woman, Culture, and Society*. Stanford, CA: Stanford University Press, 1974.
11. C. Gilligan. *In a Different Voice: Psychological Theory and Women's Development*. Cambridge, MA: Harvard University Press, 1982.
    C. Gilligan, N. P. Lyons, and T. J. Hanner, eds. *Making Connections: The Relational Worlds of Adolescent Girls at Emma Willard School*. Cambridge: Harvard University Press, 1990.
12. Gilligan et al., *Making Connections*; Chodorow, *"Family structure and personality."*
13. Twelve Steps and Twelve Traditions! New York: Alcoholics Anonymous World Services, 1953, p. 57.
14. Narcotics Anonymous. Van Nuys, CA: World Services Office, 1982, p. 81.
15. *Alcoholics Anonymous*, p. 2.
16. E. Kurtz. *A.A.: The Story*. New York: Hazelden, 1988.

17. Kurtz, *A.A.: The Story,* p. 12.
18. D. L. Wilson. "Thomas Jefferson and the character issue." *Atlantic Monthly,* 270:5, November 1992.
19. S. Freud. "Infantile sexuality." In A. A. Brill, ed., *The Basic Writings of Sigmund Freud.* New York: Modern Library (Random House), 1938, p. 595.
20. W. Reich. *Character Analysis.* New York: Touchstone, 1945, pp. 217–224.
21. H. Ansbacher and R. Ansbacher. *The Individual Psychology of Alfred Adler.* New York: Harper, 1956.
22. A. Adler. *Social Interest: A Challenge to Mankind.* New York: Capricorn, 1964.
23. S. Forward. *Men Who Hate Women and the Women Who Love Them.* New York: Bantam, 1987.
24. R. Norwood. *Women Who Love Too Much: When You Keep Wishing and Hoping He'll Change.* New York: St. Martin's Press, 1985.
25. Dinnerstein, D. *The Mermaid and the Minotaur: Sexual Arrangements and Human Malaise.* New York: Harper and Row, 1976.
26. N. Chodorow. *The Reproduction of Mothering.* Berkeley: University of California Press, 1978; Gilligan, *In a Different Voice.*
27. A. G. Kaplan and J. P. Bean. *Beyond Sex-Role Stereotypes: Readings Toward a Psychology of Androgyny.* Boston: Little, Brown, 1976.
28. J. Larkin. *The Reshaping of Everyday Life: 1790–1840.* New York: Harper & Row, 1988, p. 193.
29. Larkin, *The Reshaping of Everyday Life,* p. 199.
30. Larkin, *The Reshaping of Everyday Life,* p. 200.
31. A. de Tocqueville, cited in E. Rothman, *Hands and Hearts: A History of Courtship in America.* Cambridge, MA: Harvard University Press, 1987, p. 91.
32. Rothman, *Hands and Hearts,* p. 92.
33. Rothman, *Hands and Hearts,* p. 92.
34. Rothman, *Hands and Hearts.*
35. C. Bronte. *Jane Eyre.* New York: Viking Penguin, 1966 (first published 1847), p. 280.
36. Bronte, *Jane Eyre,* p. 281.
37. T. J. Schlereth. *Victorian America: Transformations in Everyday Life, 1876–1915.* New York: HarperCollins, 1991.
38. E. Carpenter. *Love's Coming-Of-Age.* London: L. N. Fowler, 1896, p. 31.
39. M. C. Stopes. *Married Love.* New York: Eugenics Publishing, 1918, pp. 17, 28.
40. *Love's Coming-Of-Age,* p. 93.
41. Stopes, *Married Love,* p. 1.
42. R. Liswood. *A Marriage Doctor Speaks Her Mind About Sex.* New York: E. P. Dutton, 1961.
43. D. W. Hastings. *A Doctor Speaks on Sexual Expression in Marriage.* Boston: Little, Brown, 1966.
44. G. Flaubert. *Madame Bovary.* New York: Penguin, 1950 (first published 1856), p. 35.

45. Flaubert, *Madame Bovary,* p. 292.
46. Flaubert, *Madame Bovary,* p. 8.
47. D. H. Lawrence. *Lady Chatterley's Lover.* New York: New American Library, 1959 (first published 1928), p. 231.
48. R. N. Bellah, R. Madsen, W. M. Sullivan, A. Swidler, and S. M. Tipton. *Habits of the Heart: Individualism and Commitment in American Life.* Berkeley: University of California Press, 1985.
49. K. Thompson. "What men really want: an interview with Robert Bly." *New Age* Magazine, May 1982.
50. Kurtz, *A. A.: The Story.*
51. See "Bill's Story" in *Alcoholics Anonymous.*
52. Bill W. "Tradition two." *Grapevine,* January 1948.
53. *Alcoholics Anonymous as a Social Movement.*
54. F. S. Fitzgerald. *The Crack-Up.* New York: New Directions, 1956, p. 76.
55. J. Lever. "Sex differences in the games children play." *Social Problems,* 23:471–483, 1976.
56. D. Tannen. *You Just Don't Understand: Men and Women in Conversation.* New York: Ballantine, 1990.
57. R. J. Solberg. *The Dry Drunk Syndrome.* Center City, MN: Hazelden, 1970.
58. J. Kerouac. *On the Road.* New York: Viking Penguin, 1957.
59. R. M. Pirsig. *Zen and the Art of Motorcycle Maintenance: An Inquiry into Values.* New York: Bantam, 1975.
60. P. Matthiessen. *The Snow Leopard.* New York: Viking Penguin, 1978.
61. W. L. H. Moon. *Blue Highways.* New York: Houghton-Mifflin, 1991.
62. *Twelve Steps and Twelve Traditions,* p. 37.
63. *Alcoholics Anonymous,* p. 60.
64. Ansbacher and Ansbacher, *The Individual Psychology of Alfred Adler,* p. 47.
65. Matthiessen, *The Snow Leopard,* p. 43.
66. Kurtz, *A.A.: The Story,* p. 100.
67. *Twelve Steps and Twelve Traditions,* p. 132.
68. *A.A. Grapevine,* January, 1948.
69. R. Bly. *Openings and Limitations* (audiotape). St. Paul, MN: Ally Press Center, 1989.
70. S. J. Bergman. *Men's Psychological Development: A Relational Perspective.* Wellesley, MA: Stone Center, 1990.
71. M. McGoldrick, J. K. Pearce, and J. Giordano. *Ethnicity and Family Therapy.* New York: Guilford, 1982.
72. B. Lopez. *Arctic Dreams: Imagination and Desire in a Northern Landscape.* New York: Bantam, 1988.
73. Matthiessen, *The Snow Leopard.*
74. R. Erdoes. *Crying for a Dream.* Santa Fe: Bear & Co., 1990, p. 46.
75. J. Nowinski. *Substance Abuse in Adolescents and Young Adults: A Guide to Treatment.* New York: W. W. Norton, 1990.
76. *Narcotics Anonymous.* Van Nuys, CA: World Services Office, 1982.
    Narcotics Anonymous, p. 111.

77. *Twelve Steps and Twelve Traditions.*

78. H. Arendt. *The Human Condition.* Chicago: University of Chicago Press, 1958.

79. H. S. Sullivan. *The Collected Works of Harry Stack Sullivan, M.D.*, vol. 1. New York: W. W. Norton, 1953, p. 266.

80. H. S. Sullivan. *The Interpersonal Theory of Psychiatry.* New York: W. W. Norton, 1953.

81. J. B. Miller. *Toward a New Psychology of Women.* Boston: Beacon Press, 1976.

82. T. M. Keane. "PTSD in Men." Paper presented at *On Men: The Burdens of Masculinity,* Cambridge, MA, December 1992.

83. *Alcohol and Health.* Rockville, MD: U.S. Department of Health and Human Services, 1990.

84. D. Gilmore. *Manhood in the Making: Cultural Concepts of Masculinity.* New Haven: Yale University Press, 1990.

85. Matthiessen, *The Snow Leopard,* p. 150.

86. Matthiessen, *The Snow Leopard,* p. 152.

87. T. T. Williams. *Refuge: An Unnatural History of Family and Place.* New York: Pantheon, 1991.

88. Williams, *Refuge,* p. 94.

89. B. Whiting and C. P. Edwards. "A cross-cultural analysis of sex differences in the behavior of children aged three through eleven." *Journal of Social Psychology,* 1973, 91:171–188.

Acknowledgments

I would like to express my appreciation to my editor, Margaret Zusky, for her commitment to this project and for her careful and thoughtful editing. This book is much better for it. I would also like to express my thanks to Ruth Wreschner for her encouragement and perseverance on my behalf.

The ideas presented here have evolved over a period of years and have been influenced throughout that time by my conversations and relationships with many men. I would like to express my gratitude to them for their interest and openness.

Index

Addiction: case examples, 3–19; criteria for, vii; defining, vii; feelings associated with, 16–19; recovery from, 135–136; rituals and traditions and, 97–98

Adler, Alfred, 21, 61, 120

Adolescence, identity and: banding versus bonding, 73; case example, 73–75; learned through fathers, 71–72; peers and, 72, 76; personal inventory of, 75–76; possessions and, 72

Adolescent subculture, 98

Advertising, impact of mass, 103

Alcoholics, case examples of, 3–7, 9, 13–16

Alcoholics Anonymous (AA): "Big Book," 17; creation of, 9; group conscience in, 42–43, 82–83; twelve-step program of, vii, viii

Alcoholics Anonymous, 42

Alcoholism, emotional restraint and, 37–38

Amish, 107

Androgyny, 23

Anger, competition and, 42

Apprenticeship/apprentices: defining, 111; making a commitment to, 113–114; personal inventory of, 112; trainees versus, 111–112

Arctic Dreams (Lopez), 94

Arendt, Hannah, 103

Attachment, identity and: case examples, 83–89; personal inventory of, 90–92; relational orientation and, 89; role of experience, 87–89

Attacking, intimacy and, 140–141

Banding versus bonding, 73

Bergman, S. J., 90

Bly, Robert, 87

Bovary, Emma, 33

Bronte, C., 25–26, 32

Carpenter, Edward, 27, 28

Collaborative work: examples of, 107–110; types of, 110–111

Communication: man's resistance to, 121–123, 134–135; role of, 75. *See also* Intimacy

Competition/competitive: case examples showing conflict between the need to be different and, 43–46; entrepreneurs and, 40; insecurity and isolation and, 41–50; pressure to be, 39–40; socialization of, 32